The Impacts of Dog Tag Inc.

A Mixed-Methods Exploration of an Entrepreneurial
Fellowship for Veterans, Military Spouses,
and Military Caregivers

STEPHANIE BROOKS HOLLIDAY, KATHRYN E. BOUSKILL, SARITA D. LEE

This research was
sponsored by Dog Tag Inc.

 EDUCATION AND LABOR

For more information on this publication, visit **www.rand.org/t/RRA1898-1**.

About RAND

The RAND Corporation is a research organization that develops solutions to public policy challenges to help make communities throughout the world safer and more secure, healthier and more prosperous. RAND is nonprofit, nonpartisan, and committed to the public interest. To learn more about RAND, visit www.rand.org.

Research Integrity

Our mission to help improve policy and decisionmaking through research and analysis is enabled through our core values of quality and objectivity and our unwavering commitment to the highest level of integrity and ethical behavior. To help ensure our research and analysis are rigorous, objective, and nonpartisan, we subject our research publications to a robust and exacting quality-assurance process; avoid both the appearance and reality of financial and other conflicts of interest through staff training, project screening, and a policy of mandatory disclosure; and pursue transparency in our research engagements through our commitment to the open publication of our research findings and recommendations, disclosure of the source of funding of published research, and policies to ensure intellectual independence. For more information, visit www.rand.org/about/research-integrity.

RAND's publications do not necessarily reflect the opinions of its research clients and sponsors.

Published by the RAND Corporation, Santa Monica, Calif.
© 2022 RAND Corporation
RAND® is a registered trademark.

Library of Congress Control Number: 2022916006
ISBN: 978-1-9774-0977-5

Cover image: Courtesy of Dog Tag Inc.

About This Report

Entrepreneurial programs for veterans, military spouses, and caregivers are an important means of ensuring their successful societal reintegration following military service. Dog Tag Inc., based in Washington, D.C., offers an entrepreneurial fellowship for veterans who have served following September 11, 2001; spouses of military service members and veterans who have served since 9/11; and caregivers of these service members and veterans.

The overarching goal of this research was to provide Dog Tag Inc. with a richer understanding of how its fellowship program shapes the careers and life trajectories of its alumni. To do so, we drew on existing quantitative data on Dog Tag Inc. alumni outcomes and qualitative findings to revise an alumni survey to more adequately and meaningfully capture the longitudinal impacts of the Dog Tag Inc. Fellowship Program. We then fielded two waves of the revised survey, the results of which are presented here and complemented by qualitative data. In addition to providing valuable information to Dog Tag Inc. as the organization continues to expand and refine its programming, these findings are likely to be of interest to other organizations serving veterans, spouses, and caregivers.

RAND Education and Labor

This study was undertaken by RAND Education and Labor, a division of the RAND Corporation that conducts research on early childhood through postsecondary education programs, workforce development, and programs and policies affecting workers, entrepreneurship, and financial literacy and decisionmaking. This study was sponsored by Dog Tag Inc.

More information about RAND can be found at www.rand.org. Questions about this report should be directed to Stephanie Brooks Holliday (holliday@rand.org) and Kathryn E. Bouskill (bouskill@rand.org), and questions about RAND Education and Labor should be directed to educationandlabor@rand.org.

Acknowledgments

We are grateful to the former and current staff at Dog Tag Inc. for their tireless engagement and assistance with the RAND team. In particular, we would like to thank CEO Meghan Ogilvie, Claire Witko, Lolly Rivas, Jaime Freeman, Sarah Abu-Sheikha, Lisa Novick, and Maureen Devine-Ahl for their helpful assistance with facilitating this research. Terri Tanielian, Special Assistant to the President for Veterans Affairs within the administration of President Joe Biden, was instrumental in making this research possible and served as RAND's point of contact with Dog Tag Inc. Terri has been a terrific mentor to many at RAND and an influential motivator of positive change in policies to improve veterans' health and well-being. We would also like to thank librarians Sachi Yagyu and Anita Szafran for their steadfast help with the literature on this complex topic.

Ultimately, our gratitude goes to the many veterans, spouses, and caregivers who generously and graciously gave their time to share their perspectives and experiences with us. Whether it was through completing a survey or a conversation while walking around Georgetown, you have made this project more rewarding than we could have imagined. We are grateful to you for your service and for the many ways you continue to make a positive difference for our country.

Summary

U.S. veterans who served in the military after September 11, 2001, their families, and those who serve as their caregivers have faced significant challenges. Among them are the challenges of reintegration to civilian life, particularly at a time in which the economy is in flux and the long-term sequelae of mental and physical health issues continue to unfold. Finding new opportunities for personal and professional growth is a key aspect of the reintegration process.

Focus of the Study

Dog Tag Inc. is a nonprofit organization based in Washington, D.C., with the mission to help U.S. veterans who face service-connected disabilities, military spouses, and military caregivers "build resilience, find renewed purpose, and forge community beyond the military" (Dog Tag Inc., undated-b). The Dog Tag Inc. Fellowship Program is a five-month entrepreneurial program that fosters the development of an entrepreneurial mindset through experiential learning while emphasizing holistic wellness. The program combines university-affiliated coursework with hands-on entrepreneurial experience. Since its first cohort graduated in 2014, the fellowship program has grown considerably. Dog Tag Inc. staff remain in regular contact with most of their more than 100 alumni fellows. Staff have surmised that the impacts of the Dog Tag Inc. fellowship might extend beyond helping veterans secure entrepreneurial, educational, and employment opportunities post-military, to also promoting personal and social well-being, and it is with this hypothesis that Dog Tag Inc. leadership approached the RAND Corporation with the research question of how to more holistically understand and assess the impacts of the Dog Tag Inc. fellowship. In an initial phase of this study, RAND worked with Dog Tag Inc. to revise its alumni survey through a review of the literature, qualitative interviews and focus groups with alumni, discussions with Dog Tag staff, and cognitive interviews with a sample of alumni to test the revised survey instrument. RAND then fielded two waves of the revised alumni survey.

This report presents qualitative and quantitative insights of the impacts of the fellowship on Dog Tag Inc. alumni. The qualitative data were collected through focus groups and interviews with fellows. These findings contributed to the development of a revised alumni survey, which more directly assesses the impacts of the fellowship as expressed by fellowship alumni. We then fielded two waves of the revised alumni survey over two years to quantify the impacts of the fellowship. This report begins by briefly reviewing the existing literature depicting some of the challenges faced by post-9/11 veterans, military families, and military caregivers. It follows with in-depth findings from qualitative data collected through focus groups and interviews. The bulk of the report is centered on findings from the alumni survey. It concludes with an overview of the findings and recommendations for Dog Tag Inc. and other programs offering services to veterans, their spouses, and their caregivers.

Key Findings

Review of the Literature on Veteran Reintegration

Recent literature identifies significant challenges faced by veterans who have served in the era since September 11, 2001, their families, and those who care for them. Key among these are the difficulties inherent to acculturating back to civilian life, rebuilding one's identity, finding one's purpose, and seeking fulfilling and meaningful work. Women veterans, spouses, and caregivers also face unique and differential challenges. Another layer to the challenge are the barriers that veterans often face in accessing care and services to help overcome challenges of reintegrating into civilian life, which can spill over into adverse impacts for families and caregivers. Programs such as Dog Tag Inc. are seeking to meet an important need of the post-9/11 military community, but there is a dearth of systematic data collection on program outcomes. In this way, Dog Tag Inc.'s mission (and that of this research project) is unique within the military and veteran programming space.

Focus Groups and Interviews

The qualitative portion of this research, which consisted of focus groups and interviews with 48 alumni fellows, provided a more complete picture of the perceived impact of the program and the continued needs of alumni fellows. Fellows described their initial transitions back to civilian life as challenging, with several feeling apprehensive about joining the workforce and struggling with reclaiming a sense of identity. Fellows described a variety of motivations and expectations in starting the fellowship, from trying to regain their footing following severe health challenges to wanting to hit the ground running and flesh out an existing business idea. Despite the heterogeneity across fellows in each cohort, fellows reported a strong sense of solidarity within their cohorts and with the "Dog Tag family" more broadly. Several fellows were candid about the mental health issues that they had faced and how the fellowship had helped bring them out of a desperate place. Fellows also described finding more confidence in advocating for their own needs and in networking. Fellows' definitions and understandings of personal success also shifted, with many fellows underscoring the importance of giving back to their communities (including the veteran community) and making personal and professional steps forward, no matter how small.

Revised Alumni Survey

We also fielded two waves of a revised version of the alumni survey, developed by RAND in collaboration with Dog Tag Inc. through a previous project. We had 67 respondents complete the survey in 2020 (55-percent response rate) and 87 in 2021 (57-percent response rate). Most of the survey respondents were employed at least part-time. It was most common for respondents to work for a company (about 46 percent in 2020 and 37 percent in 2021), but some alumni were pursuing entrepreneurial pathways (about 22 percent in 2020 and 32 percent in 2021), often while they were employed in other positions or pursuing education. Interestingly, in 2021, substantially more fellows were pursuing postsecondary education (including degree, certificate, or other training programs). In the first year of the survey, nearly half of respondents reported that they were underemployed, but that number had dropped to about 30 percent in 2021, which may reflect some of the impact of the coronavirus disease 2019 (COVID-19) on the job market, or perhaps the shift to postsecondary education.

In the revised survey, we asked more explicitly than in the previous version of the survey about the ongoing impacts of the fellowship on areas such as personal growth, self-acceptance, and finding a sense of identity. For most items in both years, we found that more than 40 percent of respondents reported that the fellowship continues to affect these areas to a moderate or great extent. Responses to other items highlighted the myriad ways that the fellowship has benefited the personal and professional lives of fellows, including helping them to take the next steps to pursue their personal goals, helping them to clarify their professional goals, giving them the tools needed to pursue new professional opportunities, and helping them approach their professional life in a more flexible way. Since completing the fellowship, an increasing number of fellows have pursued additional education or training, and about half have been serving their communities through their work, education, or volunteering. Many reported that they are working on a business idea—with about half of those working on the idea they began as a fellow. Moreover, fellows continue to stay engaged through the alumni programming. Overall, survey responses highlight the high levels of satisfaction that fellows have with their fellowship experience. More than 94 percent of fellows reported that they are satisfied or very satisfied with the program, and fellows reported being extremely likely to recommend the fellowship to a friend.

Conclusions

This project elucidated the professional and personal impact of the Dog Tag Inc. fellowship through both qualitative and quantitative methods. There were certain limitations to the study—for example, there may be selection bias in the fellows and alumni who opted to participate in focus groups and interviews or complete the survey. There was also a gap between when the quantitative and qualitative data were collected. Finally, data collection occurred during the pandemic, which has had a substantial impact on the labor market, and it is difficult to know whether the findings would be consistent with fellow experiences pre-pandemic. It is also important to keep in mind that this survey was developed to be specific to the Dog Tag Inc. fellowship, and therefore the population of fellows and alumni may not be representative of the larger population of post-9/11 veterans, spouses, and caregivers. However, our high survey response rate is a strength of the study. This project is also indicative of Dog Tag Inc.'s commitment to systematically tracking the impact of the fellowship on current fellows and alumni, especially as the organization continues to expand its program, with a new site added in Chicago with Loyola University as its anchor in 2022.

Based on our findings, we identified the following recommendations for Dog Tag Inc. (DTI) to consider as the organization continues to fine-tune, expand, and evaluate its program:

- **Continue to monitor the ways that the COVID-19 pandemic has affected the employment sector, including its effect on entrepreneurship.** The fellowship will be especially relevant if it can explicitly address these factors in its curriculum.
- **Determine what role DTI wants to play in supporting alumni, and consider offering programming, resources, or awareness building efforts to address common alumni challenges.** DTI has expanded its alumni offerings and now has a robust range of programming available to alumni. However, alumni continue to cite challenges to pursuing their goals, and DTI may use this information to identify additional ways to support alumni.
- **Consider the role of technology in the program for future cohorts.** The most recent two cohorts (cohorts 12 and 13) were offered in a fully virtual format, and fellows from these cohorts reported a positive experience. However, as of mid-2022, many workplaces are returning to in-person operations, and it will be important for DTI to weigh the pros and cons of in-person, virtual, and/or hybrid options.
- **Identify ways to maintain fidelity to the DTI model as the program grows.** As the DTI fellowship expands, program staff will face the challenge of replicating the most effective components of the program while also taking into account any unique features of the new Chicago site. Identifying a staff "champion" can be key to successful expansion of the program.
- **Find opportunities to diversify the staff of the organization and ensure their cultural competence with military populations.** Our interviews and focus groups suggested that these steps would help to ensure the comfort of all fellows.
- **Continue administering the annual alumni survey, and continue to bolster data collection at enrollment and completion of the program in a way that complements the alumni survey.** This includes adding a complementary pre-fellowship and post-fellowship survey, which will allow DTI to track fellow progress across the fellowship experience and continue to inform program improvements.

- **Perform regular focus groups and interviews, facilitated by a third party.** Qualitative data are especially well-suited to capturing rich nuance about the fellow and alumni experience, and having a third party facilitate this data collection will help to mitigate bias introduced through social desirability.
- **Explore the possibility of conducting a formal evaluation of the DTI fellowship.** The alumni survey is an important aspect of detecting the longer-term outcomes that fellows achieve. However, it can be difficult to know what outcomes were observed as a result of the fellowship versus other external factors, even when questions ask about the influence of the fellowship. A more formal program evaluation could help to further develop the evidence base for the DTI model.

In conclusion, we find the impacts of the Dog Tag Inc. fellowship to be rich, complex, varied, and evolving. Commitment to tracking the longitudinal effects of the fellowship is an important step for making programmatic improvements and helping fill the gaps in understanding how to improve the process of veteran reintegration into the workforce and society. This study also points to the importance of providing training to assist service members, veterans, spouses, and caregivers in the transition to civilian life, both in terms of employment opportunities and cultivating a post-military identity.

Contents

Figures and Tables

Figures

Tables

CHAPTER ONE

Introduction

Take a walk down Grace Street in historic Georgetown, Washington, D.C., and you will come upon a bakery in a classic row house with a conspicuous automatic sliding door. The modern-day sliding door is ill-matched to the Colonial and Federal architecture, but it hardly resembles a "24-hour pharmacy-chain location," as some locals once protested. Walk in, order a coffee and a freshly-baked pastry, and take a seat. As you look around, spot the small, square-shaped elevated platform to the right of the counter. Above it hang over 100 eye-catching dog tags suspended from the ceiling. The space is inviting, and the structure and the scene do not suggest a run-of-the-mill bakery. You might suspect that there is more than meets the eye at Dog Tag Bakery, which became well known through a nationwide sale of its brownies at Starbucks in 2018, as well as through visits from high-profile patrons, including from former President Barack Obama and Vice President Joe Biden in July 2018.

In fact, the uniqueness of Dog Tag Inc. (DTI) stretches well beyond the bakery. As the loaves of bread rise downstairs, a small, diverse group of post-9/11 military veterans with service-connected mental and physical disabilities, along with spouses and caregivers of military service members and veterans who have served since 9/11, are learning in a classroom upstairs. DTI is actually a "living business school" that empowers its fellows to rediscover their purpose and find a sense of community through a business- and entrepreneurship-centered fellowship. Twice a year, a Washington, D.C.–based cohort and a Chicago-based cohort, totaling about 16 members, are enrolled in the five-month Dog Tag Inc. Fellowship Program—an entrepreneurial program designed to accelerate reintegration into civilian entrepreneurial and employment opportunities.

DTI's program is designed to focus on each individual fellow. The DTI learning environment is intentionally small-group and immersive and encompasses a curriculum consisting of coursework in entrepreneurship, accounting, management, communications, finance, marketing, and business policy, culminating in a certificate in business administration from either Georgetown University in D.C. or Loyola University Chicago. Dog Tag Bakery serves as an incubator for the fellowship program, offering hands-on training opportunities and real-world application to the seven business fields covered in the university coursework. Alongside the business courses, there is a series of wellness activities in which fellows participate, from yoga to journaling, as well as a performance event entitled Finding Your Voice, which encourages a narrative, expressive form of personal storytelling. During the five-month program, DTI fellows complete approximately 138 hours of workshops with entrepreneurs, business leaders, and experts (known as Learning Labs); 119 hours of formal education earning their business certificate; 113 hours of hands-on learning at the bakery; 140 hours of wellness activities; and 57 hours on a capstone project, providing fellows the chance to apply the lessons learned (Dog Tag Inc., undated-a). The spirit of the program remains the core mission of its founders, Father Rick Curry (of the Society of Jesus) and Constance J. Milstein, who in 2014 set out to ensure that veterans, military spouses, and caregivers would not face limitations to pursuing their career goals. Upon completion of the program, fellows have access to alumni programming, designed to maintain the strong relationships formed during the program and provide ongoing personal and professional development.

The DTI fellowship is open to veterans who have served following September 11, 2001; spouses of military service members and veterans who have served since 9/11; and caregivers of these service members and veterans. Active service members who are within six months of their transition from military service are eligible, as are current Guard and Reserve members. Acceptance into the program is competitive, meaning there are more applicants than there are open spots. Applicants all go through an interview process. Since the fellowship launched in 2014, more than 160 veterans, caregivers, and spouses have become alumni of the DTI fellowship. To date, 67 percent of fellows have been veterans, 2 percent have been military translators, 40 percent have been spouses, and 10 percent have been caregivers, with several fellows falling into multiple groups (e.g., are both veterans and caregivers). Unique to the program is its blending of veterans with service-connected disabilities with ranks including E-3 and above and O-1 to O-6, and educational levels attained ranging from high school diplomas to doctoral degrees.

DTI leadership, working from the hypothesis that the fellowship program might be conveying benefits beyond employment status, enlisted the RAND Corporation to qualitatively explore how DTI fellows interpret the impacts that the program has had on their lives and career trajectories. In the first phase of this study, we gathered in-depth, qualitative feedback from DTI alumni so as to understand the perceived value of the program in their own words. We then incorporated these qualitative insights into revisions of the alumni survey to track the long-term professional and personal impacts of the program on its fellows. Then, we fielded the survey in two waves over two years.

Prompted by the community outcomes measurement framework of *A Field Guide to Ripple Effects Mapping* (Chazdon et al., 2017), DTI leadership set out to gain an understanding of how the fellowship could catalyze a series of additional benefits to oneself, one's family, and one's community. We adhered to the central aim of this approach in the first phase of our study by using an ethnographic ethos rooted in the voices and perspectives of fellows themselves and not limiting descriptions of the program's impact solely to career outcomes. The qualitative findings from the first phase of the study supported DTI's goal of reworking its existing alumni survey to more directly capture the impact of the fellowship, and then fielding this survey to alumni on an annual basis to understand the post-fellowship experience and ongoing effect of the program.

In the chapters that follow, we provide an overview of the project methodology (Chapter Two), followed by a review of the literature relating to the underlying challenges faced by post-9/11 military veterans, military spouses, and caregivers (Chapter Three). We then present qualitative findings from in-depth focus groups and interviews conducted with alumni and current fellows (Chapter Four), followed by quantitative findings from two waves of Dog Tag Inc.'s new alumni survey, developed in partnership with RAND through a previous project (Chapter Five). The final chapter presents conclusions and recommendations for Dog Tag Inc. (Chapter Six). We also include detailed appendixes presenting the complete alumni survey (Appendix A), a description of our previous work to develop the survey to ensure it was adequately capturing the expected outcomes of the fellowship (Appendix B), the underlying data for the figures in Chapter Five (Appendix C), and our analysis of an earlier version of the alumni survey, fielded prior to the present project (Appendix D).

CHAPTER TWO

Methodological Approach

Our study included several data collection methods. First, we performed an environmental scan of recent literature to understand the broader context of the military-to-civilian reintegration process for service members, spouses, and caregivers. Next, we conducted focus groups and in-depth interviews with DTI alumni to better understand their experience with the fellowship. The analysis of the qualitative data also shed light on key domains that previously had been missing from the DTI alumni survey, which was revised by RAND as part of a project preceding the present effort. This revised alumni survey was fielded twice, in fall 2020 and fall 2021. In this section, we provide details of these methods.

Environmental Scan of the Literature

The impacts of such programs as DTI are best understood in the context of the broader challenges and services available to post-9/11 veterans, their spouses, and caregivers. The literature on military-to-civilian reintegration for former service personnel is vast. However, less is known about how this process of integration affects military spouses (and families) and caregivers. In March 2020 and again in March 2022, we searched PubMed, Academic Search Complete, the Military Database, and Dissertation Abstracts using the following keywords:

> (military AND veteran?) OR "military caregiver?" OR (veteran? AND caregiver?)
> AND
> (reintegrat* OR transition* OR reentry OR "re-entry" OR readjust*).

We additionally performed a hand search for literature on the impacts on families and spouses. We omitted clinical studies relating to the treatment protocols for physical and mental health issues, non-U.S.-based military systems, and studies pertaining to veterans prior to 9/11. In addition, our literature search included only publications found in peer-reviewed journals, yielding a total of 521 articles. Although there have been multiple surveys conducted through military and veteran support organizations to assess needs and challenges with transitions by military families, it was outside the scope of this current research to assess the methodological rigor of these surveys.

One reviewer read all titles and abstracts and selected a subset of articles to depict the variety of challenges and services available to veterans, spouses, and caregivers. These articles were selected for their date of publication, methodological rigor (e.g., sufficiency of the sample size), and relevance in the following areas, which help contextualize the DTI program in the broader landscape of programs and services for veterans, military families, and caregivers: military-to-civilian transitions, high-level estimates of service-connected disabilities, available services and access to services, and challenges faced by caregivers and spouses.

Focus Groups and Interviews

The first portion of the qualitative research centered on an inaugural convocation, or alumni summit, in November 2019. The summit was open to all alumni (which, at the time, included Cohorts 1–10, or $N = 106$) and key stakeholders (e.g., donors, program instructors), and DTI had anticipated that the summit would bring many alumni back to Washington, D.C., allowing for in-person focus groups. Via email, DTI staff invited alumni who had expressed interest in attending the summit ($n = 64$) to participate in one of six scheduled focus groups in the two days prior to and the day of the summit. Half of those invited ($n = 32$) participated in a focus group.

We developed a comprehensive, semistructured focus group and interview protocol to capture a variety of experiences and perspectives among fellows. The protocol covered a variety of topics (e.g., how fellows learned about DTI; daily life pre- and post-DTI; aspirations and goals; perspectives on blending veterans, caregivers, and spouses; useful aspects of the fellowship; areas of improvement; definitions of success; engagement with DTI). The guide was refined through iterative discussions with DTI staff and findings from the literature (e.g., challenges in acculturation to the civilian workplace).

Recognizing the potential for bias among the focus group participants (i.e., those who attended the summit might be more likely to be engaged or perceive the fellowship more favorably), we recruited an additional sample of fellows from all alumni, minus those who had participated in a focus group ($n = 74$) for in-depth interviews conducted telephonically. DTI provided us with a list of additional alumni who had not previously taken part in a focus group and may or may not have attended the alumni summit, stratified by cohort (1–10), gender, demographic category (veteran, spouse, caregiver, or multiple), geographic location (a proxy for whether alumni can readily meet with DTI staff), and whether alumni had remained engaged with DTI post-graduation. It is important to note that no fellows had identified exclusively as a caregiver; that is, all nonveteran fellows identified as a spouse and/or spouse/caregiver, although these roles are often blurred. In addition, two fellows out of all ten cohorts served as translators in the military. Engagement was dichotomized as *yes* or *no*, based on whether an individual met one of the following criteria: completion of two or more alumni surveys, met with DTI fellows, interviewed fellowship applicants, or attended a DTI event in the previous year. We selected a purposive sample of possible interviewees by stratifying across cohort, gender, demographic category, location, and engagement status. We reached out to a total of 39 fellows, of whom 18 agreed to participate and two later canceled, for a total of 16 interviews. Interviews were conducted from January to March 2020. The distribution of the focus group and interview participants is discussed in more detail in Chapter Four and depicted in Table 4.1.

We recorded the focus group meetings and had them professionally transcribed. We recorded the interviews, when consent was given by the interviewee, while taking detailed written notes (nearly verbatim). We referred to recordings for accuracy when needed. The transcripts and notes were uploaded into Dedoose, a qualitative data-analysis software program that facilitates team-based coding (SocioCultural Research Consultants LLC, 2020).

We developed a codebook based on the questions covered in the interview protocol, specifically those that captured the impact of DTI and the challenges that alumni have faced before, during, and after the fellowship. Each transcript was coded independently by a member of the research team trained in qualitative methods and with an expertise in the topic to identify key themes. The identification of themes followed a two-stage analysis approach (Butler-Kisber, 2010), including a coarse-grained phase to broadly classify emerging themes and a more detailed phase in which themes were identified by frequency repetition and use of metaphor and through exemplary descriptions (Ryan and Bernard, 2003).

Alumni Survey

As part of a previous project in 2019–2020, RAND worked with DTI to revise its alumni survey. Though DTI had fielded an alumni survey previous to that effort, DTI leadership was concerned that the existing items did not capture the true impacts of the program on participants. The complete revised survey instrument appears in Appendix A, and the process of revising the survey is detailed in Appendix B. In this section, we provide an overview of the survey administration and content.

We administered the revised web-based alumni survey twice, in fall 2020 and fall 2021. Each time, the survey was open approximately four to five weeks. DTI provided contact information and basic demographics (e.g., gender, location) for all its alumni at each survey wave. In 2020, a total of 121 alumni were invited to participate, and in 2021, a total of 151 were invited to participate. The RAND Survey Research Group sent personalized invitation emails and survey links to all alumni, with weekly reminders until the survey closed. Each respondent was assigned a study ID to maintain confidentiality of participants. Participants received a $15 gift card for completing the survey. in total, 67 individuals completed the survey in 2020 (55-percent response rate) and 87 completed the survey in 2021 (58-percent response rate).

Table 2.1 summarizes the content of the survey. The versions of the survey fielded in 2020 and 2021 were largely the same, though slight changes were made to the 2021 survey based on input from DTI. For example, one item assessed the alumni activities that respondents had participated in since completing the fellowship, and the response options were updated to reflect the most current alumni activities in 2021. In addition, response options were added to several items to assess ways in which the coronavirus disease 2019 (COVID-19) pandemic had affected respondents or the ways that the program helped fellows navigate challenges related to the pandemic.

We analyzed data from both the 2020 and 2021 waves of the survey. Our primary analyses were largely descriptive in nature. We examined the number and percentage of individuals endorsing each response

TABLE 2.1

Survey Domains and Items

Survey Domain	Number of Items
Impact of COVID-19 on personal and professional life	2 items (2020 only)
Employment status and underemployment	4 items (2020); 5 items (2021)
Demographic characteristics	4 items (2020, 2021)
Perceptions of current employment or postsecondary educational experiences	8 items (2020, 2021)
Perceived effect of fellowship on personal and professional life	12 items (2020); 13 items (2021)
Enriched Life Scale (Genuine Relationships, Sense of Purpose, Civic Engagement, Global Enrichment)	30 items (2020, 2021)
Post-fellowship experiences (education, civic engagement, work toward business idea, participation in alumni activities)	7 items (2020, 2021)
Pursuit of goals	2 items (2020, 2021)
Overall satisfaction with fellowship	2 items (2020, 2021)
Open-ended feedback	1 item (2020, 2021)

option for categorical items, and we computed the mean and standard deviation (SD) for continuous items. In 2020, we performed some exploratory analyses examining differences by cohort and location, but we found little difference in responses based on these categories; therefore, we do not report these data, and we opted not to perform these analyses using the 2021 data.

We conducted two types of formal hypothesis testing when examining the results. In 2021, we compared respondents who completed the program when it was fully in-person to those who completed the program when it was fully virtual, because we expected that there might be some differences in the post-fellowship experience of these two groups. We used chi-square tests for categorical variables and independent sample t-tests for continuous variables. These analyses focused on questions regarding underemployment, pursuit of additional education, perceived effect of the fellowship on personal and professional life, the Enriched Life Scale (Angel et al., 2020), post-fellowship work toward a business idea, and overall satisfaction. In addition, we conducted a series of longitudinal analyses focused on the subgroup of respondents who participated in both the 2020 and 2021 survey waves ($n = 44$). We conducted a descriptive analysis of changes in underemployment status from 2020 to 2021 in this group. In addition, we explored whether there were statistically significant changes in responses from 2020 to 2021 in this subgroup using repeated measures t-tests (note that for these analyses, we treated the five-point response scale as a continuous variable to allow us to conduct repeated measures tests). Our longitudinal analysis focused on items related to perceived effect of the fellowship on personal and professional life, the Enriched Life Scale, and overall satisfaction with the fellowship.

CHAPTER THREE

What Challenges Do Veterans, Caregivers, and Spouses Face in Transitioning from Military to Civilian Life? Insights from the Literature

Veterans transitioning from military to civilian life—as well as their spouses, caregivers, and family members—face a variety of social, economic, mental health, physical health, and relationship issues in their search for a new normal. The U.S. Department of Veterans Affairs (VA) has described *reintegration* as assuming roles within one's family, community, and place of work following separation from the military (VA, Veterans Health Administration, 2010). A Pew Research Center study found that nearly half of the veterans who served in the first decade following 9/11 had a particularly challenging return to civilian life in terms of financial, emotional, and professional strain; this statistic worsens for veterans who experienced a traumatic life event, served in combat, were seriously injured while serving, or were married while serving (Morin, 2011). More devastating is the "deadly gap," or the increased risk of suicide observed among transitioning veterans compared with other veterans, which is compounded by barriers to psychiatric care and general issues with reintegration (Sokol et al., 2021).

Securing employment is a critical aspect of a veteran's successful reintegration to civilian life; however, veterans can struggle to find their footing in the civilian labor market and often lack guidance and support in translating their military skills into civilian employment (Wewiorski et al., 2018; Stern, 2017).

Although post-9/11 veterans are often described as a homogenous group, it is important to note that their reintegration experiences can vary widely based on their military experiences, education, branch of service, gender, and post-military place of residence (rural versus urban settings) (Vick, 2020). In addition, post-9/11 veterans are the most diverse population among all combat eras with respect to race, ethnicity, and gender (VA, Office of Data Governance and Analytics, 2017; VA, National Center for Veterans Analysis and Statistics, 2018). As the post-9/11 wars in Iraq and Afghanistan have come to an end, more attention has been given to "veterans in transition" (Biniecki, Yelich, and Berg, 2020) and the subsequent challenges of reintegration, but also to how businesses and institutions of higher education can better understand the advantages that veterans can bring.

It is important to note that the literature is decidedly focused on experiences of veterans, as opposed to caregivers and spouses, but it is evident that military caregivers and spouses need to be factored into a broader understanding of military-to-civilian transitions (Ramchand et al., 2014). Additionally, most studies focus on highly populated states with large metropolitan areas, indicating a potential gap in understanding the experiences of more rural veterans and their families (Van Slyke and Armstrong, 2020).

Military-to-Civilian Transitions

Military culture is rife with social expectations, norms, values, and identity shifts, which can lead many to experience "reverse culture shock" upon returning to civilian life (Angel et al., 2018; Orazem et al., 2017;

Erwin, 2020; Becker et al., 2022). Recent data show that the proportion of veterans reporting poor health and well-being outcomes may increase over time after separation (Vogt et al., 2022). The social disconnect stems in part from the differences between military culture and American civilian culture; the former emphasizes collective goals and action, self-sacrifice, obedience, loyalty, conformity, humility, and mutual support (Mamon et al., 2020; Ainspan, Penk, and Kearney, 2018; Demers, 2011), which stand in contrast to the individualistic, independent, opportunistic values espoused by American civilians (Mamon et al., 2020).

Furthermore, estimates show that a third of veterans hold a military identity as their primary identity (Kelty, Woodruff, and Segal, 2017), a finding which is not unique to the United States (Flack and Kite, 2021; Tarbet, Moore, and Alanazi, 2021). Additional qualitative research has shown how planning for one's post-military life is dependent on how tied the veteran remains to their military identity; the stronger the military identity, the less planning for reintegration they tend to do (Kleykamp et al., 2021). Developing a "coherent personal identity" lends itself to a stronger sense of purpose and direction in one's life, in addition to better mental and behavioral health outcomes (Meca et al., 2021). In a qualitative study of veterans experiencing the transition to civilian life, veterans described the need to find a new purpose and expand their identities outside the military, while also noting the perceived stigma of asking for help with the transition (Shue et al., 2021).

These cross-cultural clashes carry over into educational settings (Dyar, 2019; Borsari et al., 2017; Gregg, Howell, and Shordike, 2016) and the workplace, with veterans reporting a lack of social camaraderie with nonveteran coworkers and a lack of a sense of urgency in terms of completing work tasks among nonveterans (Strong, Crowe, and Lawson, 2018), as well as frustration with having to perform skills that are not as advanced as one's tasks in the military (Harrod et al., 2017). Alternatively, civilians "typecast" veterans as possessing strengths in planning and executing tasks but lacking interpersonal skills and emotional intelligence (Shepherd, Kay, and Gray, 2019). However, a greater sense of social connection to civilian coworkers has been associated with life satisfaction among post-9/11 veterans (Senecal et al., 2019), which might indicate that helping veterans and their nonveteran coworkers overcome stereotypes and build mutual understanding is an important goal.

Challenges to the veteran-to-civilian employment transition include "civilian employer's military job knowledge deficit, veteran anxiety with civilian employer's lack of clearly defined new-hire processes and civilian employer misunderstanding of veteran compensation, benefits and family involvement expectations" (Dexter, 2020). In a 2020 study, nearly half of veterans surveyed reported that reintegration into the civilian workplace was very difficult (Hunter-Johnson et al., 2020). A systematic review found that a large majority of the literature reported the need for employment among veterans, but that veterans reported that employers stigmatized veterans for mental health issues and the disconnect between military and civilian job skills (Van Slyke and Armstrong, 2020).

As a result, some post-9/11 veterans have reported experiencing a loss of solidarity and reduced trust with civilians in their struggle to reintegrate (Senecal, 2018). Others have experienced a lack of, or loss of, social support and increased social isolation (Gorman et al., 2018). Furthermore, there is evidence to suggest that civilians might carry an implicit bias that veterans are unstable (Schreger and Kimble, 2017). This cultural rift has highlighted the importance of support group participation for veterans, transition groups and programs for military family members and friends to learn how best to support veterans and each other, and increased military cultural competence among providers of health care and services for veterans and their families (Demers, 2011).

Several studies have found that the experience of reintegration to civilian life might be particularly pronounced among women veterans, whose challenges—including disadvantaged upbringing, military sexual trauma, and the strain of being a minority group in the military—can make it more difficult to reclaim their identity in civilian life (Williams et al., 2018; Boros and Erolin, 2021; Vogt et al., 2020). This is in part because women must also include an occupational gender identity, meaning that women have both identities in the workplace and outside the workplace, which is not readily a concern for their male counterparts (Greer, 2020).

Other unique groups include military officers and infantry veterans, who may face particular challenges related to adaptation to civilian employment, especially after decades of experience and leadership within the military (Biniecki, Yelich, and Berg, 2020; Minnis, 2020). However, recent research shows that certain demographic groups face additional challenges in reintegration, including Army veterans (as compared with Marine Corps, Navy, and Air Force veterans), younger veterans, and those living in rural areas (Vick, 2020).

Although the majority of existing research on reintegration focuses on the veterans themselves, family members also face a diverse and complex set of challenges in the process (Gil-Rivas et al., 2017). Reintegration approaches that incorporate and enhance family and community relationships and draw on peer support are increasingly important in the transition from military to civilian life (Ainspan, Penk, and Kearney, 2018).

Service-Connected Disabilities

The underlying challenges of acculturation can be exacerbated when a veteran and a veteran's family are coping with posttraumatic stress disorder (PTSD), traumatic brain injury (TBI), and/or other visible and invisible wounds of war (McGarity et al., 2017). Co-morbid mental health conditions are also common; in a recent multisite study, over two-thirds of post-9/11 combat veterans with PTSD also had major depressive disorder (Goetter et al., 2020). Sadly, veterans transitioning to civilian life have a higher risk for suicide compared with service members and other veterans who are more established in the civilian world (Ravindran et al., 2020; Sokol et al., 2021).

A recent national sample of newly separated veterans showed that 53 percent reported chronic physical (e.g., musculoskeletal) ailments and 33 percent reported mental health disorders (e.g., anxiety, depression, PTSD) (Vogt et al., 2020), which is consistent with VA utilization and diagnostic data (VA, Veterans Health Administration, 2010). Vogt et al., 2020, also found that these conditions were more pronounced among enlisted personnel than officers and were particularly pronounced among men and women who had deployed to warzones. Depressive symptoms and PTSD were found to be higher among women veterans (Freedy et al., 2010). Women veterans experience worse mental health outcomes, on average, than both civilian women and male veterans (Williams et al., 2018). A recent study also found that although both men and women are in need of health care for anxiety, depression, and sleep-related issues, women veterans may be less likely to receive such care from VA than men (Copeland et al., 2020).

Veterans who perceive ostracism or who are feeling socially ignored or excluded may also face worsened deployment-related psychological issues, such as anxiety and psychological distress (Wesselmann et al., 2018). Stigma persists as an issue to treating mental health issues among post-9/11 veterans (Botero et al., 2020). These findings underscore the importance of having a supportive and accepting social environment to foster not only reintegration but also mental health and well-being. In addition, mental health practitioners for veterans must be in tune with the additional stress brought on by the process of reintegration (Stevenson, 2020).

Services Available to Ease the Transition to Civilian Life

All U.S. service members, regardless of branch, are required to participate in programming upon service separation to assist with reintegration to civilian life (e.g., education, employment, access to benefits, housing, health care, and fostering social support) (Gettings et al., 2019), although it is important to note that this requirement has been enacted only recently. VA also offers vocational services and understands employment as an important aspect of community reintegration (Wewiorski et al., 2018). A recent nationwide survey found that over 50 percent of veterans transitioning back to civilian life used an employment-related service or program shortly following discharge (Perkins et al., 2020). Another recent survey found that veterans are seeking employment counseling above and beyond services that are offered upon separation from the military (Derefinko et al., 2019).

VA programs that provide skills learning and gradual exposure to everyday tasks have been beneficial to veterans with disabilities, although concerns remain about whether veterans would lose their disability benefits if they were employed and about a lack of accommodations in programs and employment for veterans with disabilities (Shepherd-Banigan et al., 2021). Additionally, newly separated veterans with mental and behavioral health issues, such as PTSD, TBI, and depression, rarely access employment services and vocational rehabilitation through VA and other programs (Davis et al., 2020). This emphasizes the importance of having interventions for post-9/11 veterans with co-morbid mental health conditions that focus on successful reintegration and foster social support (Goetter et al., 2020).

Data on outcomes from the thousands of public and private programs and services offered to veterans are scant (Perkins et al., 2020). Recent skills-matching analyses revealed that programs that help veterans directly apply military skills to civilian occupations are warranted, yet more research is needed to understand the optimal process for helping veterans cultivate new skills and seek employment outside their military training (Schulker, 2017). A recent intervention tested a career coaching program against standard employment services and found that those who participated in the coaching program had increased employment earnings, and mental and physical health over a year later (Bond et al., 2022). An additional trial is underway through VA (Davis et al., 2020), thus giving promise to the effectiveness of career interventions; however, it is worth noting that VA-led interventions will not reach the many post-9/11 veterans who are not connected to VA care, or their caregivers and spouses.

Veteran entrepreneurship and self-employment have been identified as an important area to explore with respect to veteran reintegration. The latest data show that up to 60 percent of veterans were employed within their first 90 days following separation and that half of these veterans reported use of online job databases and job application programs (Perkins et al., 2020). A 2017 study found that successfully self-employed veterans are more likely to report greater resilience, purpose in life, altruistic service to other veterans, and general gratitude (Heinz et al., 2017). The literature on the role of traumatic life events in career transitions is also growing. An early multiple case study among soldiers and marines highlighted the importance of "reestablish[ing] assumptions of the world and self" when individuals face traumatic events (e.g., a military combat-related event that causes medical discharge) and have to chart out new career paths (Haynie and Shepherd, 2011).

Providing support to augment self-efficacy is important, particularly for veterans with disabilities. A recent study of entrepreneurs with disabilities, the majority of whom are veterans, found a positive correlation among entrepreneur- and disability-support programs on perceptions of self-efficacy (Tihic, Hadzic, and McKelvie, 2021). A 2020 review article written primarily by post-9/11 veterans underscored the importance of having veteran service organizations collaborate with other stakeholders and provide peer-to-peer support among veterans (Geraci et al., 2020). In addition, support to enhance veterans' self-work and identification of skills is recommended to assist with the transition from military service to civilian work (Krigbaum et al., 2020). Narrative accounts of the transition to civilian life identified key areas for programs and the public alike to keep in mind: "understand deployment hardships; appreciate deployment accomplishments; assist veterans in getting professional help; listen, do not judge; and recognize that employment is critical to reintegration" (Sayer et al., 2021). Lastly, programs that offer direct mentorship to translate military skills into the civilian workplace led to more success for veterans seeking employment (Perkins et al., 2022). For veterans struggling with the transition from military service member to rehabilitation patient to contributing member of one's home and community, there is promise in therapeutic approaches that emphasize explorations of self-identity (Grimell, 2017) and incorporate storytelling and narratives (Linstad and Schafer, 2020). Expressive writing interventions also might be beneficial with respect to facilitating reintegration, social support, and general health and functioning (Sayer et al., 2015).

Caregivers and Spouses

Family members of veterans also are affected by challenges of reintegration to civilian life (Derefinko et al., 2019). Although many do successfully navigate the challenge of reintegration, experiences among military families differ and can be challenging for military spouses (Sayers, 2011). Long-term family dysfunction, exacerbated by mental health challenges and high caregiver or spousal burden, is an unfortunate reality (Link and Palinkas, 2013). In contrast to the vast literature written on veterans' transitions out of service, little attention has been given to veterans' spouses, who are also experiencing a significant transition to a post-military life (Keeling et al., 2020).

Caregivers of post-9/11 veterans with brain injuries also face significant stress from stigmatization, which is also correlated with depression, anxiety, and loneliness, among a host of other negative outcomes (Phelan et al., 2018). An unfortunate but not altogether surprising finding is that depression among women military spouses was positively correlated with the degree of reintegration difficulty faced by a veteran spouse (Knobloch, Basinger, and Theiss, 2018).

Military spouses, particularly women, face deficits both in securing employment and in their earnings vis-à-vis civilian peers (Meadows et al., 2015). Post-9/11 caregivers (many of whom are spouses) have higher proportions of unemployment than do pre-9/11 and civilian caregivers and noncaregivers (Ramchand et al., 2014).

Summary

This brief environmental scan depicts significant challenges faced by post-9/11 veterans, military spouses, and military caregivers with respect to reintegration to civilian life, navigating the workplace, and managing physical and mental health issues. Employment-focused programs and programs that emphasize self-identity work might be an important means of easing the transition from military to civilian life. However, outcome data on such programs and services are sparse, which emphasizes the need for more systematic data collection. Identifying the challenges faced by these populations—and specific subpopulations, such as women veterans—also is critical for understanding the importance of DTI fellowship outcomes. Finally, the literature review helped guide the survey revision, particularly in regard to identifying knowledge gaps with respect to the trajectories of veterans, military spouses, and caregivers and providing a source of candidate measures that have been validated in both civilian and military populations.

CHAPTER FOUR

How Dog Tag Inc. Alumni Describe the Program's Impact: Qualitative Findings from Focus Groups and Interviews

Prior to drafting the revised alumni survey, we set out to understand how Dog Tag Inc. alumni fellows (referred to in this chapter simply as "fellows")—the veterans, spouses, and caregivers who have graduated from the program—describe the impacts the program has had for their personal and professional lives in their own words. Both Dog Tag Inc. and the RAND research team hypothesized that the program offered positive impacts beyond gaining proficiency in entrepreneurial skills, and this exploratory data collection sought to understand these broader impacts and reasons why they might have been experienced differentially among alumni and across cohorts. These qualitative findings also contributed to the revision of the alumni survey by expanding the types of questions and responses included.

The findings in this chapter are from six focus groups among 32 fellows (conducted in November 2019) and in-depth interviews with 16 fellows, conducted from January to March 2020. The focus group and interview participants represent all cohorts, all types of fellows (e.g., veteran, caregiver and/or spouse, multiple roles), and variation in geographic locations of fellows. The number of participants in each focus group ranged from two to nine. The distributions of the focus group and interview participants are shown in Table 4.1.

As described in the methodological approach chapter (Chapter 2), all fellows identified as veterans, military spouses, military spouses/caregivers, veterans/spouses, or veterans/spouses/caregivers. Of the 64 alumni who had planned to attend the alumni summit in November 2019, 32 joined a focus group (participation rate = 50 percent). In addition, we contacted 40 alumni as part of recruitment for interviews; 16 agreed to participate (participation rate = 40 percent).

The subsample of fellows that took part in either a focus group or an interview largely reflects the total population of fellows, although the focus groups skewed female[1] and to more-recently graduated cohorts, which can be attributed to the fact that the alumni summit coincided with Cohort 10's graduation, and several members of the graduating cohort opted to join the focus groups. Lastly, one-quarter (*n* = 4) of the fellows who participated in an interview were characterized as *non-engagers*, meaning that they have not had substantial contact with DTI staff, attended alumni events, or completed the alumni survey post-graduation. The aim of including non-engagers was to try to reduce response bias among the qualitative study participants.

The focus group and interview protocol guided fellows through a semistructured discussion on a variety of topics, including journeys of learning about DTI and expectations of the fellowship, perspectives of being in integrated groups, experiences throughout the fellowship, definitions of success, perceptions of the "Dog Tag family," and career experiences post-DTI. Because of the similarity of the themes presented in both the focus groups and the interviews, the findings are interwoven throughout the chapter without direct men-

---

[1] In 2020, 60 percent of alumni were women.

TABLE 4.1

Fellows Included in Focus Groups and Interviews

Fellow Characteristics	Alumni Fellows (*n* [%])
Cohort	
1	1 (2%)
2	2 (4%)
3	6 (13%)
4	4 (8%)
5	3 (6%)
6	6 (13%)
7	2 (4%)
8	3 (6%)
9	8 (17%)
10	13 (27%)
Type of fellow	
Spouse/caregiver	14 (29%)
Veteran	30 (63%)
Veteran/spouse or veteran/ spouse/caregiver	4 (8%)
Geographic location	
DMV[a]	41 (85%)
Outside DMV	7 (15%)
Gender	
Male	15 (32%)
Female	33 (68%)

[a] *DMV* colloquially refers to the region including Washington, D.C., Maryland, and Virginia.

tion of whether they came from focus groups or interviews. This is a deliberate choice to protect the confidentiality of those who participated in the study, because DTI knew which fellows had taken part in the focus groups. Omissions of details, such as specific career choices or life circumstances, as well as personal grievances with the alumni experience, also have been made to ensure confidentiality. This chapter presents the various themes tied to the key hypothesis of our study—specifically, that the fellowship confers benefits above and beyond learning entrepreneurial skills. The findings are organized chronologically; overviews of how fellows came to join the program are provided first, followed by their experiences during the fellowship, and, finally, how they perceive the impacts the program has had on their personal and professional trajectories.

Arriving at Dog Tag Inc.

Daily Life Before Dog Tag Inc.

Alumni fellows were asked at the beginning of an interview or focus group to describe their day-to-day lives prior to starting the DTI fellowship. Although fellows have diverse backgrounds and experienced their transitions in vastly different ways, a common thread across responses to this question was that their transitions were seldom smooth.

Some fellows were in a holding pattern, not knowing whether they or their spouses could be called back to active duty. Although some had anticipated retirement from the military, others saw a sudden end to their or their spouse's military career, leading to periods of time in which these individuals and families were, in the words of one fellow, "really shaken up." The suddenness of a departure from the military was described by one fellow as "heartbreaking." Another veteran fellow emphasized that "When you leave [the military], you're on your own!" And another described "being responsible for so many people and a huge budget" while leading military projects, "and then you're just responsible for yourself." Being responsible for oneself, especially after being part of the collective "mission," also made for a rougher transition. In the words of one veteran fellow,

> After I retired from the military 100 percent, I really had to ask myself, "Do I really want to do on the civilian side what I did in the military?" Because I not only have medical issues, like physical—pretty major-league medical stuff, but there is a PTSD component, and I can have some pretty dramatic things. And so I had to really kind of say, "No." So, I wasn't actively looking for anything.

Some fellows also described feeling "burned out" from their previous careers and wanted to find a more fulfilling next path in their lives.

Some fellows had already sought additional educational or vocational training and wanted to set their newfound skills in motion within a new career. One veteran fellow described wanting to leverage the entrepreneurial spirit that he had cultivated while being stationed around the world and flesh out his various business ideas. Several spouse fellows described finding career options that were feasible within the constant relocations required of military families. One veteran fellow had been performing shift work throughout the night to make ends meet, the product of being unable to identify work that met his skills and qualifications.

Suffice it to say, spouses, caregivers, and veterans alike found difficulty in the "What now?" questions that are ushered in with transitions. One veteran noted, "I was struggling with directional decision. I couldn't really get together enough concentration of effort and motivation to really meaningfully pursue anything." Another caregiver/spouse fellow added, "I was consumed with being a caregiver and a stay-at-home mom. I had not known who I was for so many years, and what I wanted to do, and what my visions and goals were." Another added, "Everything was focused on the husband and the kids. [I was] trying not to be depressed and all of that." Another fellow echoed this in stating, "[I was] dealing with fires, figuring out how I was going to pay my bills, take care of our kids, deal with my emotional roller coaster and the intimidation of going back in the workforce. I used to pride myself in my ability to get out there and sell myself, so to speak."

Fellows described varying degrees of needing to attend to physical and/or mental health needs, often having to attend regular medical appointments for themselves or their spouses. One spouse/caregiver fellow recalled, "My whole life was 'go to the hospital and wait.'" Some fellows had more-severe circumstances. Veteran fellows described self-loathing. One spouse said, "I used to lock myself in a dark room" because of severe depression, coupled with unemployment and marital issues. Another spouse/caregiver fellow had "spent two years in crisis management" because of her husband's suicidal ideation. Still others faced unexpected deaths in their families, alongside being in the "throes of abusive relationships and dealing with anxiety and PTSD."

As reflected in the literature, significant mental and physical health issues compounded the difficulty of the transition for many. One veteran fellow who had experienced mental health issues said, "I just didn't have any feelings. I was checked out. I had a lot of anger towards people in general." Another added, "I found that I kept a lot of things and pushed them deep inside, sort of like an armor. . . . I just started really looking at myself in terms of who I am, so that I can carry out a business and help other people."

Connections to Dog Tag Inc.

No two experiences of connecting to DTI were the same, which might point to the variety of different touch points through which DTI recruits its fellows. These experiences ranged from hearing about DTI at a job fair in the southeastern United States to being encouraged to apply by staff at various veteran service organizations. Fellows were attracted to "the uniqueness of the program, the high-caliber Georgetown professors, and the hands-on experience." One fellow joked, "I was at a networking event, and it was the cookies that kept bringing me back," before asking DTI staff for more information about the fellowship. Some found the bakery before finding the fellowship, either having tried a Dog Tag Bakery brownie or having seen a photograph of former President Barack Obama and Vice President Joe Biden visiting the bakery in July 2018. In addition, many learned of DTI through word of mouth or social media posts from fellows (and many subsequently reported referring several others to the program post-graduation).

Transitions to Civilian Life and Considerations About Joining the Workforce

Fellows spoke of the difficulties of transitioning back to civilian culture—specifically, the stark distinction between core military and civilian value systems. One fellow was attracted to one DTI staff member's pitch that the program was "bootcamp for the civilian world."

There are clear preconceived notions and fears that hinder the process of acculturation. To veteran fellows, civilians were "scary," and "everyone is about themselves, and they'll double-cross you and stab you in the back—veterans are not used to that." Fellows also spoke of the damaging preconceived notions and misunderstandings that civilians have about people affiliated with the military. One veteran fellow elaborated on this, stating,

> I served honorably for . . . [many] years. Then, when we're done, we're placed back in this society with 99 percent of people who have no idea how we've lived, how we've been traumatized, and we're expected to thrive. How do you do it? You don't! We've seen evidence of that with the 24 members who commit suicide every day. I'm the gray house on the block of 99 blue houses. And the blue houses say, "Why can't you just paint yourself blue?" We are depicted as people who are damaged, or they get their understanding of us from television. That, in and of itself, is a re-traumatization. It's like a secondary trauma of my experience of having to leave everything behind.

Several fellows mentioned differences in values regarding self-promotion as a source of difficulty. They felt that it is boastful to talk about one's individual strengths, a skill integral to obtaining employment in American culture, when the military emphasizes the collective mission and maintaining humility. One veteran fellow said, "I was still using military lingo. You're not supposed to boast about yourself. It was hard for me to talk myself up, and I still didn't really know who I was. Was I a . . . [military rank]? Or was I . . . [name]?" Another added, "We're taught not to glorify ourselves. . . . It's incredibly hard to shake that! It feels wrong! It felt awful to the point that I would get a rumble in my stomach when I had to talk about myself." Networking small talk "with a bunch of fakeness is, ugh, exhausting. It's draining," said one fellow. Another was "baffled" at how people in D.C. professional circles could "blow their own horn so eloquently."

Fellows also mentioned common practices in U.S. professional culture that are antithetical to the military. For example, making off-the-cuff decisions without oversight from leadership was a source of concern for fellows, especially after being in a context "where things are scripted and structured." Using social media also was seen as a source of stress for some, especially those who had been working in classified environments and had no "footprint online." Those who had worked in secure environments (i.e., on classified work) found the transition particularly isolating because they cannot speak to their family, friends, or potential employers about the reality of their lives and work in the military.

Spouses and caregivers also found the process of acculturation to be challenging. One veteran fellow added, "As a warrior, we only sort things in black or white, but as a civilian, we operate in the gray." Speaking about the broader impact on military families, one spouse described the "longitudinal impacts" that military families face in enduring continuous transitions, including leaving friends, neighbors, and classmates and having a parent return from being deployed and then redeploy. "The military only trains you for *right now*," she added, before elaborating on the long-term challenges of reintegration. Lastly, it was difficult to identify direct ways to translate one's experiences as a spouse and caregiver into the workplace, which led to some feeling apprehensive, or, as one spouse fellow noted, "My outside-the-home résumé stacks up to [that of] a 22-year old, but I'm middle-aged. It sort of seemed like a nightmare, so I would avoid it."

Motivations and Expectations About Starting the Fellowship

Fellows expressed a variety of motivations and expectations in anticipation of starting the fellowship. Some fellows had very clear plans for developing an entrepreneurial project and were "looking forward to the journey" and the "the time to figure out [my business ideas]."

Several others were drawn to the opportunity to learn the ins and outs of running a business and to carry forward the passion they had put into developing an initial idea. Other fellows felt motivated by their own missions. For example, one veteran fellow "liked the idea of helping other veterans and thought Dog Tag would introduce . . . [me] to other veterans who were doing the same." Many had some inkling of a business idea and felt comfortable with "figuring out a bit better what it was I wanted to do."

Some were outright skeptical about what they would get out of the program but admitted that the fact that it would result in a certificate from Georgetown University meant that it likely wouldn't be for naught. Others found it appealing that the educational program would not contribute to existing student debt.

Several described DTI as a "bridge" and a source of stability after having "moved all over the place, all the time." One veteran fellow explained, "I was just looking for an empowering environment to take me from my recent transition out of the military and to really, kind of, develop what's next." Another veteran fellow echoed this sentiment:

> I spent the majority of my life as a veteran and have done extensive research on why we have difficulty transitioning back to society. I was lucky enough to have a job that was translatable from what I did in the military into the civilian sector, but I still felt lost. I didn't have a job where I felt like a valuable member of society. I wouldn't use the word *value* in terms of pay, but in terms of me feeling like I was a person who could be a part of that organization. I learned about DTI and was so happy that they accepted me. They care so much and they want it to be a soft place to land where we can be, and we can be understood, while we can simultaneously be introduced to life outside the military in a way that didn't harm us or set us back.

Others admitted that they "didn't have a friggin' clue," wanted to build more structure into their day, or "needed help getting unstuck." One person added, "My entire adult life has just been one transition after another, and I kind of lost myself in the role of a military spouse. As . . . [my spouse] was separating [from the military] . . . I knew I had an opportunity to start what I wanted to do again and not just fill the space while we were at his particular duty station." It is important to consider that reclaiming that identity is no small feat. As one veteran fellow said, "I had heard from other people who had gone through the program that it helped them find their identity and get back on their feet. The motivation was to get back on my feet again." Reflecting on the motivation question, one fellow remarked, "I think one of the beautiful things about the program is that you realize you're not alone—there is no smooth transition—and that what you're going through is normal."

Thus, fellows fell somewhere on a spectrum from needing to regain their footing first before developing a career path, to needing a springboard and concrete tools with which to set their projects into motion.

Perspectives on the Fellowship

Fellows were asked a series of questions related to the components of the fellowship. These questions pertained to fellows' perspectives on integrating veterans, caregivers, and spouses; useful aspects of the curriculum; areas of improvement; and surprising aspects of the fellowship.

Integrated Groups

One interesting aspect of DTI is the fact that it blends together veterans, spouses, and caregivers, all with the goal of leveling the playing field and removing the hierarchy that is intrinsic to military life. It is also important to note that many fellows occupy two or three of these roles, operating as both a veteran and spouse and/or caregiver.

Fellows were asked explicitly about what it was like to "leave military rank 'at the door,' so to speak." One veteran fellow poignantly noted that "it was the first time that people that I went to see every day called me by my first name." Nearly all fellows found this to be a positive aspect of the fellowship or eventually came to see it as such. Some said that it "made no intuitive sense at first." For one fellow, "it was a huge problem" that he and his cohort overcame through communication. One formerly high-ranking fellow reflected on how the experience led him to understand the need to empathize and communicate with others in his cohort. He added,

> I learned a lot from leaving rank at the door. It was not that difficult, because it was almost ten years later when I joined [the fellowship], but still, I defaulted back to being in a military mindset. . . . Some became leaders. I wanted everyone to succeed. My lesson learned was that everyone has different journeys of getting to their destination, and you should know more about their journey before you expect that they should be on the same page as you. It's really about communicating—finding out what's really going on.

There were natural leaders in each cohort who described having to play a leadership role without necessarily acting like an officer. As one fellow noted, "Half the people in the room are not military, and you have to deal very differently with them. Honestly, it keeps things in check." Another added, "there's an openness and vulnerability in working with peers." This process was equally important for spouse and caregiver fellows, who described feeling a sense of intimidation due to being alongside former officers.

Integrating groups, however, was noted to be rife with skirmishes and tense moments (i.e., fellows did not always get along with one another). But ultimately, fellows respected that the meaning of the fellowship was beyond their individual personality clashes. One veteran fellow couched his perspective on how well the integrated groups worked in terms of whether a veteran clung deeply to their military identity as their sole persona or whether they saw other aspects that define who they are. He added, "There are a lot of people who let . . . [their rank] define them. I never felt like anybody in the Dog Tag group ever wore their rank. It was a good mix." Interestingly, several fellows believed that DTI staff were very deliberate in selecting the right mix of fellows, and that the fellows placed trust in that decision.

Some participants described the integrated groups as liberating, especially those who had less-than-favorable experiences in the military. One fellow noted that diversity within the group was never "the primary topic of discussion or the thing that defined any of us," meaning that individual differences were not called out within the cohort. Another fellow added, "It's the expectations set from Dog Tag and the way . . . [the fellowship] is structured. It wasn't a division of branches of service, which could sometimes be divisive, or officer/enlisted, or spouse or whatever. It was just like, 'We are Cohort X, and that's it!'" Still, one fellow who had retired from the military a decade prior to the fellowship was seeking reconnection and a sense of mutual understanding from those who also had been deeply entrenched in military culture. Ultimately, many fellows described the integrated groups as accepting, challenging, and as much a part of the transformational process as any other aspect of the fellowship.

Integrating groups also helped veterans and spouses/caregivers cultivate compassion within their cohort and in their lives. One fellow who was in the midst of a divorce noted,

> Through the fellowship, I learned so much more about how the military made [my husband] lose himself. . . . I wouldn't have known that unless I was with . . . [my cohort] every day and all day talking about just what the military is. . . . So, I have a lot more compassion for him and respect for myself. I was the military spouse.

Another veteran fellow enthusiastically replied, "It had never occurred to me how much military spouses do, at least the wives—in particular, the stay-at-home moms. . . .These women are so creative. It's amazing!" Another echoed this response in stating, "It changed my narrow-mindedness about military spouses." Another veteran fellow added,

> It's helpful to see what my wife might be going through. . . . Certainly, my 'leftovers' are her leftovers. There is great freedom in being able to talk to a wife that is not your own about issues that are similar, right? It gives different levels of understanding. If there isn't that mix, that can't happen.

Still, it might be important to note that one fellow complained that the fellowship seemed to be shifting away from combat veterans to spouses and caregivers and would have hoped that DTI would keep veterans as the core component and focus of each cohort.

Useful Aspects of the Fellowship

The curriculum afforded the opportunity to learn and develop a skill set in business operations. Because of the diverse background and experience of the fellows, fellows reported a variety of aspects of the fellowship that they found to be most useful. For some, the most useful aspect was developing public speaking or networking skills, and for others, it was concrete skills, such as grant writing. Additional fellows spoke of "developing the soft skills," such as cultivating social intelligence, creativity, and flexibility within networking and communicating. Others noted the benefits of adding to their list of professional contacts and expanding their network, particularly through Learning Lab guests.

Fellows appreciated the mix of on-the-job-training and classroom learning. Learning Labs were a useful middle ground of translating classroom experience into real-life examples. As one fellow remarked about the usefulness of Learning Labs, "[Instructors] have worked out the kinks and done all the hard work, and then [come to us with], 'Here, we want to share our knowledge with you;' you don't have to suffer the things that are easily fixed and are kind of just the same across the board." Another added that the Learning Labs introduce fellows to "different approaches, experiences, and success stories—and stories that are still in progress. And I think you find what resonates with you."

Fellows also mentioned the consistent coaching from multiple program representatives. Describing the program as "high-touch," fellows talked about how "You get it [coaching] from various people in the organization, from the CEO [chief executive officer] to everyone below, in operations. Everyone knows your name and your situation. . . . You get feedback and tips. Guest speakers invest their time in you. I didn't know to expect it but really came to appreciate it. It's coaching at a rigorous level." Taken together, the business curriculum and the coaching helped one fellow "sharpen . . . [his] mentality to go into small business and gave

. . . [him] the tools to utilize those skills in the future—not only the baseline business courses at Georgetown but also the networking and coaching and having people help you and think through the steps of building your business."

In retrospect, fellows recalled, "Now that I'm done with the program, the wellness—the holistic aspect—is what resonates, more than the other aspects. The emotional-intelligence skills are far more valuable than any other." This points to the duality of the program's focus—the "nuts-and-bolts" curriculum side and the "personal, introspective" side.

Finding Your Voice

When asked to reflect on the most useful aspects of the fellowship, fellows frequently highlighted Finding Your Voice—a culminating event during which fellows perform a personal narrative—even though, at the start, several thought "it was a complete joke," "dreaded it," or "thought it was pointless, a colossal waste of time." Men, women, veterans, spouses, and caregivers all appreciated this aspect of the program, and, for many, it was the first time they had been immersed in narrative storytelling. As one veteran fellow remarked, "The Marine Corps does not ask you to reflect." One veteran fellow noted, "There were battles that I had covered up. . . . With Finding Your Voice, I uncovered the past me to find the future me." One veteran fellow elaborated,

> Finding Your Voice—I call that my significant emotional event. It was one of those where it was snot bubbles, crying, ugly crying, like, what is going on right now? That surprised me the most. Truly peeling back my own onion and figuring out who I am outside of the uniform. It was hard because I had let myself become the uniform. It was my identity. Taking it off, I lost myself, and that was just damn hard to come to grips with!

Another veteran fellow, who wondered if he was "in the right place" when the fellowship introduced mindfulness and well-being components into the curriculum, said:

> I thought, "It can't hurt. I'll give it a shot." Finding Your Voice was so powerful. And for me, too. In that setting, for the most part, the others were veterans or spouses, and it was so powerful to share with them my story and my struggles. And afterwards, it felt . . . it's hard to explain. There was a lot of growth there, a ton of growth there. It just felt liberating. Just shared a lot of stories that I normally wouldn't have shared, but I felt totally comfortable with sharing them. I thought, "This isn't normal for me," a guy, and the military did a great job telling me to put up these walls, stonewall my feelings, and then I felt comfortable letting my stuff out. Letting out the past trauma from before the military—and for a very long time, I didn't want to admit it, but when you talk about day-to-day life, people don't know that, they don't see that. You can't come here and act like that trauma didn't affect you in some way. You can't fool yourself; it did affect you. It helped me grow and express a lot of that. I had that realization that there's some stuff that I needed to talk to someone about it.

This fellow went on to talk about how his experience was a catalyst for helping him seek long-overdue therapy.

Fellows were candid, speaking about childhood sexual traumas and deep experiences of being deployed. One recalled opening up about her suicidality vis-à-vis the pressure to keep a stiff upper lip instilled through military culture and her upbringing. "It was the first time I'd felt calm in a year, and to say that aloud and have it be absorbed in that way was really powerful," she said. In that sense, Finding Your Voice is a risk—fellows are asked to speak openly about their life circumstances and experiences in front of their peers and fellows from other cohorts. Although intense, difficult topics are discussed, everyone emphasized how they were met with empathic and considerate responses.

One fellow recalled Dog Tag cofounder Father Curry's mantra that "the stage is as important as the oven in the bakery." Another fellow said succinctly that "without Finding Your Voice, you don't have Dog Tag."

Finding Your Voice is part of the fellowship's broader emphasis on wellness. Although those who had yearned for more concrete business skills reported that "we could have done less of the frou-frou side of things—the mindfulness, the well-being," others said that the mindfulness exercises and Find Your Voice were "so unique and instrumental." One fellow added, "You learn how to regulate your emotions on a day-to-day basis. Decisionmaking, relationships—professional and personally. A lot of people give lip service, but they really backed it up. I was so amazed. Everything they say is happening. Each individual makes the best out of it that they put into it." The wellness aspect of the curriculum helped one fellow shed light on the "need for time and a little compassion." Another explained how the program "is never about limiting yourself; it's about finding out, what are your limits?" In other words, the program deliberately aims to meet fellows "where they are," and part of the wellness curriculum helps fellows essentially meet themselves where they are with more compassion and grace. This theme is described in more detail later in this chapter.

Suggested Improvements

Fellows were asked about areas where they felt that DTI could improve its curriculum and general approach. Although all had some form of constructive criticism to offer, all were quick to note that it did not detract from their overall positive impressions of the program. Other fellows who were in earlier cohorts added that they have seen DTI staff strive to respond to criticism and change course throughout the life course of the program.

Several fellows felt as though the level of detail covered in the business curriculum was generalizable but inadequate for truly having enough applied knowledge to start a business. As one fellow noted, "I don't think we learned as much practical, takeaway knowledge as I assumed that we were going to." Others specifically wanted more details on the legal and tax aspects of entrepreneurship. A more senior veteran fellow added, "Overall, I left the program with a lot of incomplete ideas on how to get a business up and running. It did, however, give me a background to back and understand a few things better than I had been able to before, no doubt about that." This might suggest that fellows gained enough resources through the fellowship to be able to seek out additional information independently.

In regard to the curriculum, many agreed that they needed more time to digest the material and brain-storm. As one fellow noted, "They literally decided every minute that you were there, and that sometimes felt like we were children." Fellows considered how reducing repetition across speakers and being more selective with speakers could open up more time for that reflection.

Fellows also noted a variety of programmatic aspects that they felt could improve DTI. A few fellows noted that adding more diversity in DTI leadership and on the board would be meaningful, adding, "A person of color and a man should be more of a priority." Others noted that some professors needed to be better educated in military cultural competency (e.g., learning not to slam doors). Several fellows also hoped for more-structured and more-inclusive alumni-involvement opportunities. Lastly, the stipend did not necessarily meet the cost of living for some fellows, including those who commuted and those living in the high-cost-of living D.C. area. Fellows recognized that this is a delicate topic, however, and that, although the stipend was not enough to meet the cost of living in D.C., increasing it could have implications for one's eligibility for financial benefits provided by the U.S. government.

Personal and Professional Pathways Post-Fellowship

Although the fellowship might not instantaneously lead to highly successful career prospects for its fellows, fellows expressed how it became "the foundation that will forever make a difference in my life." Fellows outlined a variety of ways in which the fellowship served as a catalyst for taking new direction in one's personal and professional life. Several talked about moving from a very "dark place" to one where "Life is pretty good!" For many, DTI set the stage for subsequent growth. Fellows had difficulty explaining the mechanics of the catalyst behind their transformation. As one fellow said, "I'd call it a personal, professional, and soul makeover, but I'm not sure how it worked." Another described it this way: "You can have one of the three E's—entrepreneurship, employment, or education. But the fourth track is enlightenment."

One caregiver fellow said, "I feel more confident. I feel better. I jumped into becoming a fellow [at another service organization]. . . . the fellowship helped me in every way possible—from camaraderie to confidence. They're not going to do it for you or hold your hand, but they're going to give you all the tools, resources, and cheerleading you need to do it." Others echoed this sentiment; one veteran fellow said he had not "been this excited for . . . [a new educational degree] in a while" and credited DTI with giving him "the skills to focus on and figure out what . . . [he] needed to set his own goals." He added the caveat, "It's hard to say, because it's several years later." Not surprisingly, fellows had a sense of a broader, collective mission—which often involved giving back to their families, communities, and veterans—that was woven into their career goals.

This section highlights how fellows perceive the impact of DTI on their professional and personal pathways. Given the diversity of the population of fellows, the themes presented are diverse and signal that fellows see these pathways as a work in progress. Nevertheless, all of the fellows who took part in our study offered several ways in which the program has enriched their lives.

Professional Applications

Fellows disabused themselves of the expectation to be running Fortune 500 companies immediately following DTI graduation. Post-graduation, several were still chipping away at their project ideas, while others had chosen to pivot to other career pathways. Many fellows were turning their passion into a successful business or at least were building an education to get them to that point. Nonetheless, fellows were staying productive and were more fulfilled than before they had started the program.

Fellows described experiencing a variety of interruptions on their paths to pursuing their business ideas, including relocation, caring for ailing family members, and taking over child care responsibilities. Some described achieving financial stability and a solid footing before exploring other entrepreneurial ventures or educational opportunities. One fellow described her evolving business as "an exercise in perseverance at this point." In addition, fellows often took jobs following graduation that they recognized were stepping-stones to a more desirable career pathway. Another fellow described leaving a position for which he felt overqualified, which in turn opened up other career avenues for him—that is, he felt confident enough in his skills to pursue higher-level work.

Several also credited DTI staff with continued hands-on support post-fellowship, often with a very quick turnaround following a request. Outreach to DTI staff and requests for assistance with reference letters, college applications, and connecting fellow alumni were reported by nearly all fellows to be very common practices. One fellow, who has since started a nonprofit, recalled, "I wasn't really confident [in my idea] at the start. They basically shaped my confidence. . . . I'm getting ready to do the tax paperwork and everything to get my business started. So not once did my vision change; it just got better." As one fellow recounted, "Leaving the program, you're ready to go any which way. You've gone through a rigorous process, and you know where you're going to go, but, more importantly, you know you've got someone to help you." DTI staff were described as "good-idea fairies" who sprinkle possible options and connect fellows to possible job opportunities but leave the work to the fellows. One fellow noted succinctly that DTI staff "helped me hold myself accountable."

Developing and sharpening networking skills also has been a significant asset of the program. Fellows who live outside the greater Washington, D.C., area described using the skills they learned through the fellowship as they built up their individual networks in new regions. One fellow described understanding the need to network as an "epiphany," especially after years of having the military dictate one's social network. Fellows also reported feeling more tactful, poised, and skilled at the art of negotiating in the workplace and in fundraising. This is important, because the concept of seizing opportunities for oneself can be, as one fellow put it, "discordant with the way the mentality of the military is shaped." Speaking directly about networking, one fellow described how

> Prior to DTI, I had never felt comfortable in crowds, anyways. But prior to DTI, I would have never gone to a networking event, even if it was important to me. Since DTI, I have gone to a few. I have even branched out and gone by myself. Will I ever be the life of the party? Probably not, but I do feel a bit more comfortable in a crowd.

For many fellows, acquiring such new skills as networking ushered in more-deep-seated transformations. As one veteran fellow explained,

> But what DTI did was genius. They structured the program to be about us and giving us the ability to get access to those things we didn't know we needed, like networking, for example. And it still feels odd to walk into a crowded room. . . . In my opinion, they did hard work to say that we were important enough for them to invest their time and give us tools that would help us succeed outside of the military. The program was designed in a way that would allow us to succeed based on what we wanted to do or what would be possible for us to do. I feel like the love and care they have for us is amazing. It was like another pseudo-family.

Several fellows touched on how the program's emphasis on networking skills has helped them build better networks of support for other veterans. Fellows are feeding veterans with goods from their farms, taking in veterans experiencing homelessness, and advocating on Capitol Hill "to tell the politicians to keep veterans at the forefront of their minds." Often, this mission has involved creating solutions and improving services for other veterans and their families in need and assisting with the transition to civilian life. Others have become more civically engaged in general. Another added, "I feed my family with . . . [my current job], but I feed my soul with serving veterans."

Personal Applications

Given the challenges that many fellows have faced (and continue to face), simply having refreshed professional and personal goals can seem monumental. Although a few fellows reported that they did not feel the need to achieve a particular goal, several noted DTI to be a "safe and supportive space," with others adding, "I'm not sure I would have been able to make the progress that I have made on my own without that type of support."

Standard measures and hallmarks of success do not always capture the magnitude of the gains described by fellows. For example, three fellows, without prompting, explicitly stated, "Dog Tag has saved my life." These are three *lives*—not job satisfaction measures or income brackets. So, even though some fellows had misgivings about not being able to run a business, fellows are volunteering, giving back, and, as one noted, "on a different journey, and I'm doing important things, too. . . . This is a very real thing, that I haven't killed myself." In the grand scheme, "It's comfort with discomfort and recognizing that you can stop and look around and listen for something new. . . . You can really ground yourself in this larger experience and stop layering judgment on what success should be and just start being open to what you get from 'discomfort.'" Although neither the fellowship nor our research set out to evaluate a reduction in suicidal thoughts among fellows, it might be important to consider the observational finding among three fellows who, during individual interviews, attributed both their renewed sense of purpose and their reconnection to their identity to a substantial increase in mental health and well-being.

Fellows also described feeling more resilient after participating in the fellowship. One fellow reflected,

> Towards the end of the program . . . I felt happy, really, with myself because I was meditating; I was journaling; I was doing my yoga every morning. I was taking care of myself every single day. When the program stopped, I started working full time, and it was very easy to jump back to the old "forget about yourself; you have to work, work, work, work." And, in addition to that, [my] private life and [my] family life had not been perfect at that time, so it was additional stress. So, in 2019, when things hit the rock bottom for me in my private life, I just go back to that time [at DTI] and ask myself, 'What happened? What was I doing to be so happy?' And once I start in again loving towards myself, taking care of myself, go there and be vulnerable . . . And that is where I have that space, that place, where I can go back and retrieve those memories and use it when life is a little harder.

Another fellow echoed this sense of resilience, saying, "If I'm getting agitated or riled up about something, I talk to myself: 'Why are you feeling like this?' I use that on a regular basis, more than anything that I've learned in Dog Tag. It's helped me to become a better person. It's helped me to be a calmer person and to understand myself more and why I react to certain things." Fellows admitted their limitations, such as struggling to overcome road rage, and took "the opportunity to reflect on the man that I am."

Others spoke of how the fellowship gave them "a launch point of self-reflection" and more confidence in "telling their story." One spouse fellow explained, "It's rough, and sometimes I feel like an imposter, like I'm failing in all areas. But Dog Tag is helping me to turn off that inner critic that lets me think I'm never enough." Another fellow spoke of the tendency to "overanalyze" that is now coupled with "giving myself more grace." Fellows spoke about the difficulty of maintaining healthy relationships in their personal lives; one fellow said, "I think Dog Tag is a good model to show what healthy relationships can look like."

Fellows also likened the option to reach out to DTI staff as a "security blanket," appreciating how "they would help at the drop of a dime." One fellow also recounted how DTI staff knew that she was facing significant issues in her family and how they "kept calling and keeping in touch. They really do that! They reach out every two months even if I'm not good at keeping in touch." Several fellows touched on the informal support offered through DTI staff post-graduation. Others were happy to liken their contact with DTI staff to that of "third cousins—family, but family with convenience." Another added, "They're not 'grading' you on anything. They're just seeing how you are and what you're doing in life," and "no judgment," "it's all about empowerment and letting us choose our destiny or what we're going to do and what your success is."

Fellows described feeling more comfortable with going outside their comfort zones, be it in networking at events or learning to take time for one's personal needs without feeling guilty, the latter being a sentiment often expressed by spouses and caregiver fellows. Another veteran fellow elaborated,

> I am a people pleaser, so I've had to establish boundaries, and Dog Tag helped me come to this realization. I think it's a massive thing, particularly for caregivers, establishing the sense of self and asserting and saying, "I can love you and still say no" or "I can love you and still allow time for myself."

Fellows also mentioned a sense of reclaiming or discovering their identities, often in relation to the cultural discordance between civilian and military cultures. As one fellow noted, "[The military] doesn't give you a chance to self-determine." A veteran fellow added, "It's made me a whole different person. I was very quiet, and now I just don't stop talking." When another fellow was asked what had surprised her the most about the fellowship, she replied,

> I was surprised that people *liked* me. I could laugh again. I used to be super funny. I got my personality back. I had been stifled at home and was around a lot of negativity all the time. Dog Tag is an extremely positive environment, and we had a fun cohort. They brought me back out!

One spouse and caregiver spoke of finding herself again:

> I had not known who I was for so many years, hadn't known what I wanted to do and what my visions and goals were. . . . Going through Dog Tag just opened up a piece of me that was closed for so long. I do have goals and dreams and ambitions, and just reopening those to find myself and what I wanted to do.

The fellowship also helped fellows reflect on their identities in the broader contexts of their lives. As one veteran fellow explained,

> I think the identity thing was huge for me because I'd been in the military for 22 years, and, even before that, kind of had a childhood where I wasn't allowed to be my own person. And so then I go into the military and couldn't be my own person. And so I was so anxious and excited to get out of the military, but I, at the same time, was very lost. . . . I give Dog Tag so much credit for the environment that they create there. And we talked about it a lot, but it just being a very safe and supportive space. And I'm not sure I would have been able to make the progress that I have made on just my own internal self without that type of support.

Fellows described how their sense of identity was crystallized through the collective camaraderie of the "Dog Tag family." One veteran described the transition to civilian life and ultimately finding DTI this way: "Well, some veterans—a lot of them—have a really hard time and struggle when they get out of the military. For me, I was sad and thought I'd be losing a part of me, and then I found another military family in Dog Tag." However, not all fellows shared in this mentality, even if they were routinely in touch with DTI staff. For example, one fellow said, "I don't go to alumni events. I can't stand some people's personalities. People put themselves on pedestals—I'm like, just put your head down and do your job, don't brag or boast. It's so 'me, me, me'—like, help out the next man!"

How Fellows (Re)Define Success

Fellows often spoke at length about how they had created a different definition of success or pivoted from earlier standards of success. After what many fellows have endured throughout their life courses—in the military, as spouses, as caregivers, and throughout the transition to civilian life—it is understandable to see stability and happiness as remarkable signs of success. With that, some fellows described modest goals, such as "not doing the same thing I was doing before Dog Tag six months from now," "keeping my head on straight," "being able to say 'no,'" "giving myself more grace," or "just doing the little things, pushing the needle forward."

Fellows credited the fellowship with helping them reformulate their definition of success. As one fellow explained, "Success is actively moving forward. Dog Tag redefined me and my definition of success. My definition even six months ago is different from what it is now. The money doesn't really matter; it's what you do for your community." Another fellow reiterated this point: "It's not necessarily financial gain. It's being comfortable and being able to open other doors to help other folks out. My mind has changed so much towards that." Fellows also contextualized their success vis-à-vis their fellow veterans. Another veteran fellow said,

I had a buddy who committed suicide. I remember when I was still on active duty, and, my last year, there wasn't a lot of joy. It was so stressful every day. Even when simple problems would come up with junior guys, it felt like they were hitting me with a ton of bricks. Even then I realized there was something wrong. I didn't have a lot of joy where I used to. I look at that now as a success. Just moving the needle forward bit by bit. Even just getting up in the morning, and the Lord has blessed me with another day on this earth. Just sharing my story.

On the whole, nearly every fellow described success as being happy, finding purpose in life, being able to create a comfortable life for their family, and making the world a better place. With that, several fellows described feeling more at ease with being flexible with new opportunities and challenges that might arise along the way.

Summary

This detailed chapter highlights both common findings and the various responses offered by 48 alumni fellows. Although fellows offered concrete criticisms of some of the programmatic and logistical aspects of the DTI fellowship, they overwhelmingly reported that their experiences as fellows and alumni were useful to their personal and professional lives. The qualitative data demonstrate that fellows arrived at the fellowship with a variety of goals and expectations and left with varying personal and professional skills. Even though not all of the fellows were pursuing entrepreneurial activities, fellows reported feeling more confident in their ability to do so.

The risk of response bias—that is, that those who participated in a focus group or interview might have more favorable perceptions of DTI than those who did not participate—might apply here; however, the 16 interviews were sampled deliberately to represent those who had not engaged substantially with DTI postgraduation. Interviewees also were made aware that DTI staff would not be made aware of their participation in an interview, so as to reduce a social desirability bias (i.e., the tendency of interviewees to provide positive feedback if they know it will be seen by the subject of the feedback). Another potential limitation is the possibility that the findings are not up to date and do not fully incorporate the challenges brought on by global events, including the COVID-19 pandemic, given that the data were collected from November 2019 to March 2020.

These findings should provide key points of consideration for DTI regarding scale-up and sustainability of the fellowship. For example, the emphasis on high-touch support and regular engagement with DTI staff requires intensive rapport- and trust-building, which is the result of having dedicated, motivated, and talented staff. Maintaining that level of support as the alumni base grows will likely require additional staff resources. This might, however, provide an opportunity for DTI to respond to the suggestion from fellows to diversify its staff, should DTI grow further or replace staff. Regardless, DTI might consider diversifying its staff and leadership going forward.

In addition, implementation science has demonstrated the importance of a intervention or program "champion"—someone who goes above and beyond to influence the relative success of the program. This role is sometimes an appointed one but can also be organically assumed by a staff member. Common characteristics of program champions include influence, ownership, physical presence, persuasiveness, grit, and participative leadership style (Bonawitz et al., 2020). These qualities can be intangible and difficult to hire for, and at times do not appear until one has been given the opportunity to express them. With program expansion and normal, cyclical turnover, it will be important for DTI to remember the influence of champions on staff and how success and impact may hinge upon the dedication and extra efforts of champions.

The personal and professional pathways described by fellows in focus groups and interviews were complex, intricate, and dynamic; in other words, the qualitative findings do not lend themselves readily to discrete, standardized survey measures and response options. Nevertheless, the following chapter reports the results of our efforts to infuse these themes into a revised alumni survey to more closely measure the impacts of the fellowship.

CHAPTER FIVE

How the Fellowship Continues to Affect Alumni and Their Post-Fellowship Experiences: Findings from Alumni Survey Data

The qualitative findings provided important insights into the experiences of DTI alumni. In turn, the survey provided an opportunity for DTI to understand how widespread these experiences are among alumni. We fielded the alumni survey twice during the course of the project, in fall 2020 and fall 2021. In this chapter, we present the findings from the alumni, including descriptive findings from each survey wave, as well as an exploration of changes over time for the subset of respondents who completed both surveys and an examination of differences in responses for respondents who completed the fellowship in person (Cohorts 1–10) versus those who had a virtual experience (Cohorts 12–13).

Participant Demographic Characteristics

In Table 5.1, we summarize basic demographic characteristics of respondents in 2020 and 2021. The majority of respondents in both years had either a bachelor's degree or higher level of education. Personal income was distributed across categories, with about 42 percent of respondents in both years reporting an income between $20,001 and $75,000. Slightly more than 50 percent of respondents in both years reported a household income greater than $75,000. About three-quarters of respondents reported living in Washington, D.C., Maryland, or Virginia (the "DMV"). Both surveys had participation from fellows across all prior cohorts.

There are some ways in which the survey respondents differ from the larger population of post-9/11 veterans. For example, about 22 percent of post-9/11 veterans have a high school diploma as their highest level of education (Gumber and Vespa, 2020), whereas most survey respondents had a bachelor's or master's degree. In addition, the median yearly earnings for post-9/11 veterans is $46,170; though we asked about income using categorical response options rather than asking for a specific number, it does appear that the income level of respondents may skew somewhat higher than this median. That said, it is also important to keep in mind that the DTI sample is a combined sample of veterans, spouses, and caregivers.

Employment Status

Table 5.2 summarizes the employment status of alumni in 2020 and 2021. When interpreting these data, it is important to note that the response options for employment status changed somewhat between 2020 and 2021 based on input from Dog Tag Inc., which was interested in more explicitly identifying individuals who identified as entrepreneurs, not just "self-employed" (for more detail, see Appendix A). Therefore, the term used for employment as a paid employee working for a company was "non-self-employed" on the 2020 survey, whereas the 2021 survey more explicitly asked whether someone was a "paid employee working for a

TABLE 5.1

Sociodemographic Characteristics of Respondents by Survey Wave

Characteristic	2020 Survey Respondents (N = 67) % (n)	2021 Survey Respondents (N = 87) % (n)
Highest level of education		
High school	0% (0)	2.3% (2)
Some college	9.0% (6)	8.0% (7)
Associate's degree	10.4% (7)	8.0% (7)
Bachelor's degree	35.8% (24)	42.5% (37)
Master's degree or higher	43.3% (29)	36.8% (32)
Other	1.5% (1)	2.3% (2)
Current personal income		
$20,000 or less	19.4% (13)	10.3% (9)
$20,001–$50,000	14.9% (10)	25.3% (22)
$50,001–$75,000	26.9% (18)	17.2% (15)
$75,001–$100,000	13.4% (9)	12.6% (11)
More than $100,000	10.4% (7)	14.9% (13)
Prefer not to answer	14.9% (10)	19.5% (17)
Current household income		
$20,000 or less	3.0% (2)	1.1% (1)
$20,001–$50,000	9.0% (6)	14.9% (13)
$50,001–$75,000	19.4% (13)	16.1% (14)
$75,001–$100,000	14.9% (10)	13.8% (12)
More than $100,000	38.8% (26)	38.6% (32)
Prefer not to answer	14.9% (10)	17.2% (15)
Marital status		
Single	25.4% (17)	23.0% (20)
Married	61.2% (41)	63.2% (55)
Living with partner	6.0% (4)	5.7% (5)
Other	7.5% (5)	8.0% (7)
Location		
DMV[a]	77.6% (52)	75.9% (66)
Other than DMV	17.9% (12)	24.1% (21)
No response to question	4.5% (3)	0% (0)

Table 5.1—continued

Characteristic	2020 Survey Respondents (N = 67) % (n)	2021 Survey Respondents (N = 87) % (n)
Cohort		
Cohort 1	6.0% (4)	2.3% (2)
Cohort 2	4.5% (3)	4.6% (4)
Cohort 3	11.9% (8)	5.7% (5)
Cohort 4	6.0% (4)	6.9% (6)
Cohort 5	7.5% (5)	3.4% (3)
Cohort 6	11.9% (8)	5.7% (5)
Cohort 7	4.5% (3)	6.9% (6)
Cohort 8	9.0% (6)	5.7% (5)
Cohort 9	13.4% (9)	9.2% (8)
Cohort 10	14.9% (10)	10.3% (9)
Cohort 11	10.4% (7)	8.0% (7)
Cohort 12	–	14.9% (13)
Cohort 13	–	16.1% (14)
Military-related experience[b]		
Veteran or translator	71.6% (48)	70.1% (61)
Spouse	34.3% (23)	40.2% (35)
Caregiver	11.9% (8)	12.6% (11)

[a] DMV = Washington, D.C., Maryland, and Virginia.

[b] Item was "check all that apply," so categories do not necessarily add up to 100%.

company." Similarly, in 2020, the survey asked whether an individual was "self-employed," whereas in 2021 respondents were asked whether they were "entrepreneurs." These terms may have pulled for slightly different concepts; therefore, it is possible that someone who considered themselves to be "self-employed" would not endorse that they were an "entrepreneur," and vice versa—though there is likely a subset of people who would use both these terms to refer to similar employment situations. Because of this change in phrasing, when comparing responses to the employment items between 2020 and 2021, it is important to keep in mind that differences may reflect a change in the percentage of alumni who were in each type of position, but might also reflect our change in terminology.

With that said, in 2020, about one-third of individuals said they had a full-time job that was not a self-employed position. In 2021, about one-quarter of individuals said they were paid employees of a company. These were the most common employment responses in each year. Fewer individuals said that they worked full-time in self-employed (2020) or entrepreneurial positions (2021) (about 12 percent and 14 percent, respectively).

In 2020, a small number of individuals reported they were employed part-time, including 12 percent in non-self-employed positions and 10 percent in self-employed positions. Those percentages were slightly

TABLE 5.2

Employment Status Respondents by Survey Wave

Employment Status[a]	2020 Survey Respondents (*N* = 67) % (*n*)	2021 Survey Respondents (*N* = 87) % (*n*)
Full-time employed		
Non-self-employed	35.8% (24)	–
Paid employee of company	–	23.0% (20)
Self-employed	11.9% (8)	–
Entrepreneur	–	13.8% (12)
Part-time employed		
Non-self-employed	11.9% (8)	–
Paid employee of company	–	13.8% (12)
Self-employed	10.4% (7)	–
Entrepreneur	–	18.4% (16)
Unemployed		
Total unemployed	28.4% (19)	–
Seeking employment	–	18.4% (16)
By choice	–	13.8% (12)
Volunteer	13.4% (9)	13.8% (12)
Postsecondary education		
Full-time	9.0% (6)	23.0% (20)
Part-time	4.5% (3)	8.0% (7)
In military transition (still active duty)	0% (0)	0% (0)

[a] Item was "check all that apply," so categories do not necessarily add up to 100%.

larger in 2021, with about 14 percent who were part-time paid employees of companies and almost 20 percent who were part-time entrepreneurs.

It is important to interpret these trends in terms of effect that COVID-19 has had on the labor market. For example, full-time workers may have experienced less disruption than part-time workers, especially in the earlier phase of the pandemic (U.S. Bureau of Labor Statistics, 2022). At the same time, in 2021, the rate of individuals quitting their jobs increased due to concerns such as low pay, lack of opportunities for advancement, and child care issues (Parker and Horowitz, 2022). We are unable to describe the specific reasons for the drop in the rate of full-time workers in our sample of DTI alumni, but these are some of the larger trends that have been observed in the labor market.

In 2020, about 28 percent of respondents were unemployed. In 2021, we asked for more detail regarding unemployment. We found that more than half of the respondents who reported being unemployed were seeking employment (16 of the 28 unemployed individuals).[1] Similar percentages of respondents reported that

---

[1] Traditionally, the term *unemployment* specifically refers to individuals who are not employed but are seeking employment. By contrast, those who are not employed and *not* seeking employment are considered to be "out of the labor force." However,

they were volunteers in 2020 and 2021. However, substantially more respondents in 2021 reported that they were pursuing postsecondary education, largely in full-time programs (23 percent in 2020 compared with 9 percent in 2021). To date, there has not been much research related to the effect of the pandemic on the percentage of people seeking additional education or job-related training in the United States. A 2020 survey found that 50 percent of surveyed adults in the U.S. were willing to retrain for a new job role (Strack et al., 2021). Moreover, a recent report from the online course platform Coursera found that the number of registered learners increased from 71 million in 2020 to 92 million in 2021; though the number of learners had already been increasing steadily since 2016, the year-over-year increases observed in 2020 and 2021 were higher than in previous years (Coursera, 2021).

Because the employment status item was "check all that apply," we were also interested in the combination of options selected by respondents at each survey wave—for example, how many were both full-time and part-time employed? The unique, mutually exclusive combinations of employment status selections are presented in Appendix Table C.1. Regarding full-time employment, most people who were full-time employed for a company did not report any other employment or educational activities (79 percent of the 24 people who reported being full-time employed for a company in 2020 and 70 percent of the 20 people who reported being full-time employed for a company in 2021). A handful reported that they were also part-time self-employed/entrepreneurs. A similar pattern was observed among those who were employed part-time for a company.

Similarly, most people who reported that they were full-time self-employed or entrepreneurs were not engaged in other employment or educational activities. It was more common for part-time self-employed individuals or entrepreneurs to endorse other employment or educational activities.

Underemployment

We assessed whether respondents considered themselves to be *underemployed*, a construct commonly used to refer to circumstances in which an individual is working less than they want to be (e.g., part-time instead of full-time) or is employed in a job that doesn't fully use their education or training (Payscale, undated-b). During the survey revision process, we learned that underemployment had the potential to affect many fellows, and there is also research suggesting that military spouses may often experience underemployment, often due to a mismatch between their level of education or skills and the employment available to them as they navigate military life (Lim and Schulker, 2010).

In 2020, about 45 percent of respondents said that they considered themselves underemployed, and 12 percent were unsure whether they were underemployed (Table 5.3). These individuals were then asked in what ways they considered themselves unemployed and were given the option to select as many options as applied. Among those, few people said that they were employed part-time when they wanted full-time work, and about one-quarter said their jobs did not fully use their education or training. The majority of respondents selected "other," filling in additional reasons they believed they were underemployed. Some reasons given by respondents included that they were in time-limited positions; that their work schedule had been affected by factors such as health, COVID-19, or family responsibilities; and that they were currently pursuing additional education or training.

In 2021, fewer individuals reported being underemployed (30 percent) and a similar proportion was unsure whether they were underemployed (12 percent). The decrease in the percent underemployed is consistent with research indicating that underemployment spiked in the early stages of the pandemic before falling to pre-pandemic levels by November 2021 (Avila and Lunsford, 2022). Among those who reported they were

---

this distinction may not be familiar to a lay audience, who might use the term *unemployed* to refer to both circumstances. Based on discussions with Dog Tag Inc., it seemed important to more explicitly ask about individuals who were and were not seeking employment.

TABLE 5.3

Underemployment Characteristics of Respondents by Survey Wave

Currently Underemployed	2020 Survey Respondents (*N* = 67) % (*n*)	2021 Survey Respondents (*N* = 86) % (*n*)
Yes	44.8% (30)	30.2% (26)
No	43.3% (29)	58.1% (50)
Unsure	11.9% (8)	11.6% (10)
If underemployed, in what way?[a]	(*N* = 38) % (*n*)	(*N* = 36) % (*n*)
Job does not fully use education or training	28.9% (11)	41.7% (15)
Working part-time but want full-time work	10.5% (4)	22.2% (8)
Underemployed due to the effects of the COVID-19 pandemic	–	13.9% (5)
Other[b]	76.3% (29)	58.3% (21)

[a] Item was "check all that apply," so categories do not necessarily add up to 100%.

[b] Other responses included working to build business full-time, including funding; pursuing further education or training; time-limited positions; work schedule impacted due to COVID-19 and associated disruptions; work schedule impacted by physical or mental health concerns; work schedule impacted by family responsibilities; and not working within preferred career field. Many responses included reference to working less than preferred (e.g., unemployed or part-time when preferred full-time work) or not using the full range of skills and/or training.

underemployed or unsure whether they were underemployed, greater percentages said their job did not fully use their education or training and that they were working part-time instead of full-time. We also added a response option to determine how many people were underemployed due to the effects of the COVID-19 pandemic, which was endorsed by 41 percent of those who were underemployed or unsure whether they were underemployed. Most respondents also selected the "other" option, providing similar reasons as in 2020.

Overall, these estimates of underemployment are not outside the range of what has been observed in other populations. A survey conducted by Payscale, a compensation data company, found that 46 percent of respondents considered themselves underemployed, mostly because they were in jobs that did not fully use their education or training (Payscale, undated-a). However, it can be difficult to provide a concrete benchmark for underemployment given the range of definitions that organizations and researchers use, with many focusing on the match between hours worked and hours desired.

Changes in Underemployment from 2020 to 2021

In an effort to understand trends in underemployment, we examined the subset of 20 individuals who responded that they were underemployed in 2020 who also completed the survey in 2021. We found that 11 individuals reported that they were still underemployed and three reported that they were unsure (Figure 5.1). However, 6 people who reported that they were underemployed in 2020 were no longer underemployed in 2021, suggesting that their employment situation better matched their personal preferences and

FIGURE 5.1
Changes in Underemployment Status from 2020 to 2021

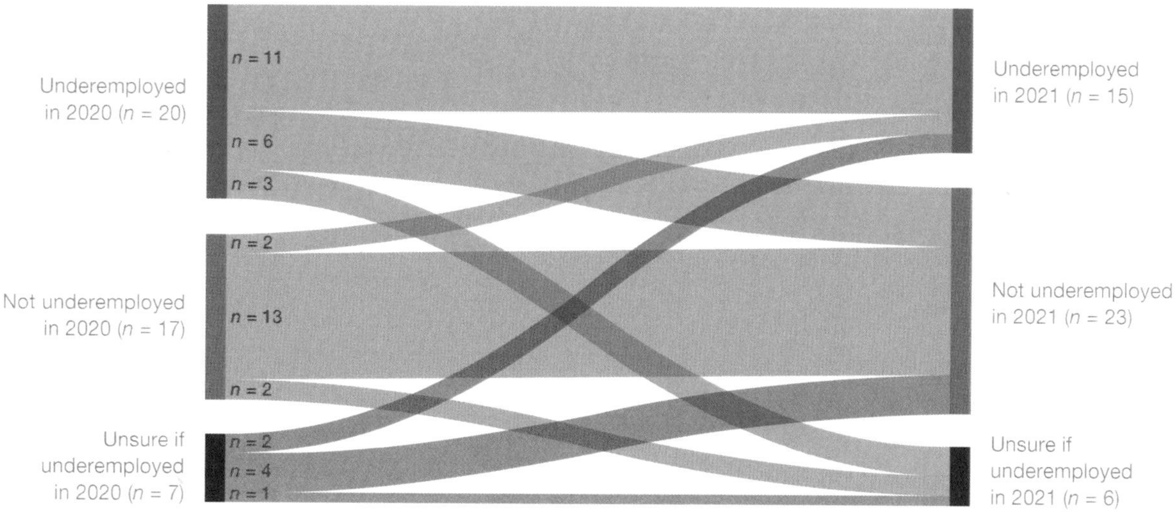

NOTE: This figure presents data on those who responded to both the 2020 and 2021 waves, so $N = 20$ does not equal the total number underemployed in the 2020 wave ($N = 30$).

circumstances in 2021 than they did in 2020. In addition, most people who were not underemployed in 2020 remained in this category in 2021.

Association Between Underemployment and COVID-19—2020 Wave

We were also interested in explicitly examining the relationship between underemployment and COVID-19. In 2020, we asked two questions regarding the impact of COVID-19 on respondents' personal and professional lives. We examined whether responses to these items were associated with underemployment (Table 5.4). We found that people who reported that their personal life had stayed about the same or had changed a little were less likely to report being underemployed, though chi-square tests revealed that these differences were not statistically significant (chi square = 7.21, $df = 4$, $p = 0.13$). By contrast, those who reported their personal life had changed a lot were more likely to report that they were unemployed. Regarding professional life, those who reported their professional life had stayed about the same were more likely to report that they were *not*

TABLE 5.4
Association Between COVID-19 Impact and Underemployment

	Not Underemployed	Underemployed	Unsure Whether Underemployed
Personal life			
Stayed about the same ($n = 7$)	71.4% (5)	28.6% (2)	0% (0)
Changed a little ($n = 21$)	52.4% (11)	28.6% (6)	19.0% (4)
Changed a lot ($n = 39$)	33.3% (13)	56.4% (22)	10.3% (4)
Professional life			
Stayed about the same ($n = 8$)	62.5% (5)	37.5% (3)	0% (0)
Changed a little ($n = 22$)	45.5% (10)	50.0% (11)	4.5% (1)
Changed a lot ($n = 37$)	37.8% (14)	43.2% (16)	18.9% (7)

underemployed. Those who reported their professional life had changed a little or a lot were somewhat more likely to report that they were underemployed or unsure if they were underemployed. However, these differences also were not statistically significant (chi square = 4.68, df = 4, p = 0.32).

Perceptions of Current Employment or Postsecondary Educational Experience

Respondents were asked a series of questions related to their perceptions of the current employment (for those who were employed at the time of the survey) and postsecondary education experience (for those pursuing postsecondary education at the time of the survey). This included questions regarding how satisfied they were with their job or educational experience, how fulfilled they felt, whether they felt comfortable advocating for themselves, and their perception of their work-life or school-life balance. Responses for each item were made on a five-point scale that was tailored to the item (e.g., extremely dissatisfied to extremely satisfied for the question regarding satisfaction; extremely unfulfilling to extremely fulfilling for the question regarding how fulfilling their work or education was). In this section, we report the percentage who endorsed the positive or very positive response for each of the items.

Current Job

In Figure 5.2, we report the percentage who reported positive or very positive perceptions of their job in both 2020 and 2021. In both years, about 70 percent of respondents indicated that they were largely satisfied with their current job, and 65 to 70 percent reported finding their job fulfilling. Nearly 80 percent reported that they felt comfortable advocating for their needs at work in 2020 and 70 percent in 2021. Over 60 percent reported that they were satisfied with their ability to maintain a healthy work-life balance. There were some slight differences from year to year—for example, in 2020, 32 percent of individuals reported that they were comfortable advocating for themselves, compared with 18 percent in 2021; however, when we examined whether there were significant changes over time for the subset of respondents who completed both survey waves, we found no statistically significant differences for any of the four items.

It can also be difficult to benchmark these findings against other data sources, as there have been different results reported across surveys. For example, a study conducted by Harris Interactive found that about 70 percent of people reported being satisfied in their job and roughly 60 percent reported being satisfied with the work-life balance offered by their employer (American Psychological Association and Harris Interactive, 2012). A 2016 reported by Pew Research reported that about 80 percent of employees reported being somewhat or very satisfied with their job, whereas a more recent Gallup poll found that, in 2021, about 87 percent of adults reported being somewhat or completely satisfied with their jobs (Gallup, undated). However, the Pew Research Center (2016) also found higher levels of satisfaction among those with higher family income and those who were employed full-time. Therefore, though the responses of DTI alumni appear to be in the general range of findings of other studies, it is important to interpret these results in the context of the larger profile of DTI alumni (e.g., the rates of full-time versus part-time employment or underemployment).

Postsecondary Education Experience

In Figure 5.3, we summarize respondent perceptions of their postsecondary educational experiences in 2020 and 2021. It is important to note that there were fewer responses to these questions in 2020 because fewer people were pursuing postsecondary education, meaning that the responses in 2020 reflect a small group of individuals. That said, perceptions of postsecondary educational experiences were also largely positive. At

FIGURE 5.2

Perceptions of Current Job Among Those Currently Employed

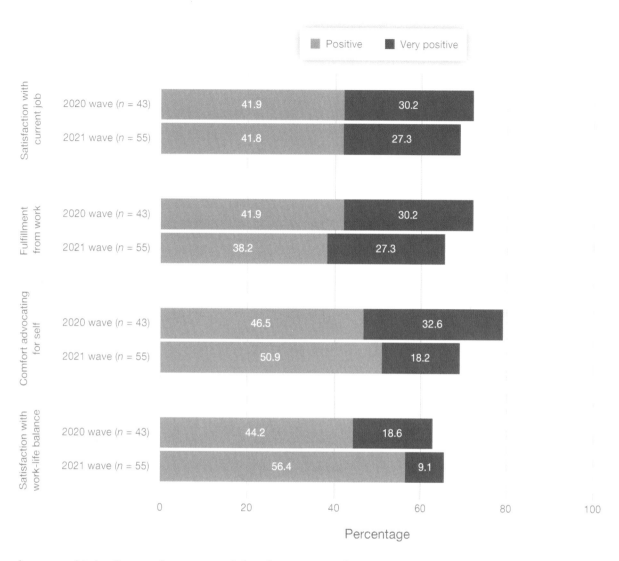

least two-thirds of respondents reported that they were satisfied with their experience in both 2020 and 2021, and nearly 80 percent reported that they found their experience fulfilling in both years. Regarding comfort advocating for themselves in their current educational experience, about 67 percent reported that they were comfortable doing so in 2020; this number had increased to 85 percent in 2021. The percentage reporting that they were satisfied with their school-life balance also increased from 56 percent in 2020 to 67 percent in 2021.[2]

---

[2] We did not conduct significance testing for the differences between 2020 and 2021 for the subset who completed both waves because of the very small number who participated in postsecondary education in 2020.

FIGURE 5.3

Perceptions of Postsecondary Educational Experiences Among Those Currently Enrolled in Postsecondary Education

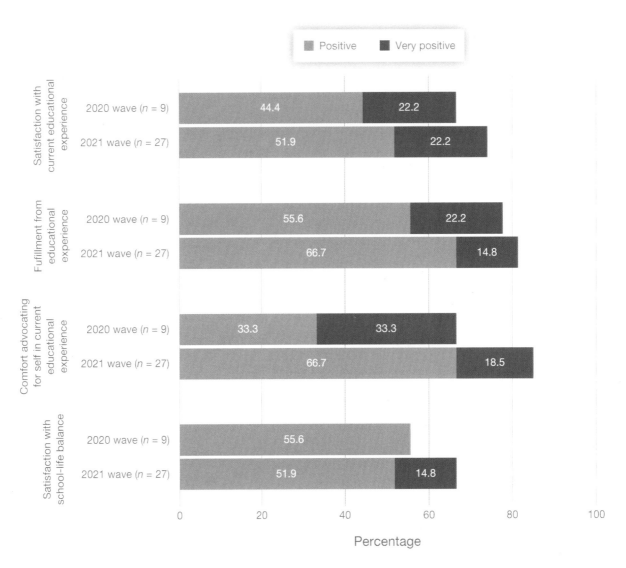

Perceived Effect of the Dog Tag Inc. Fellowship on the Personal and Professional Lives of Respondents

We assessed the perceived effect of the Dog Tag Inc. fellowship with a series of questions designed for this survey based on the qualitative data and the DTI program theory of change, which we described in this section.

Continuing Impact of the Dog Tag Inc. Fellowship

We asked fellows to report on the ways in which the Dog Tag. Inc. fellowship has continued to contribute to improvements in each of six areas of their life. Responses were made on a five-point scale and ranged from "not at all" to "to a great extent." In Figure 5.4, we report the percentage who indicated "to a moderate extent" or "to a great extent" for each item. About 45 to 50 percent of respondents reported that the fellow-

FIGURE 5.4

Ongoing Impact of the Dog Tag Inc. Fellowship

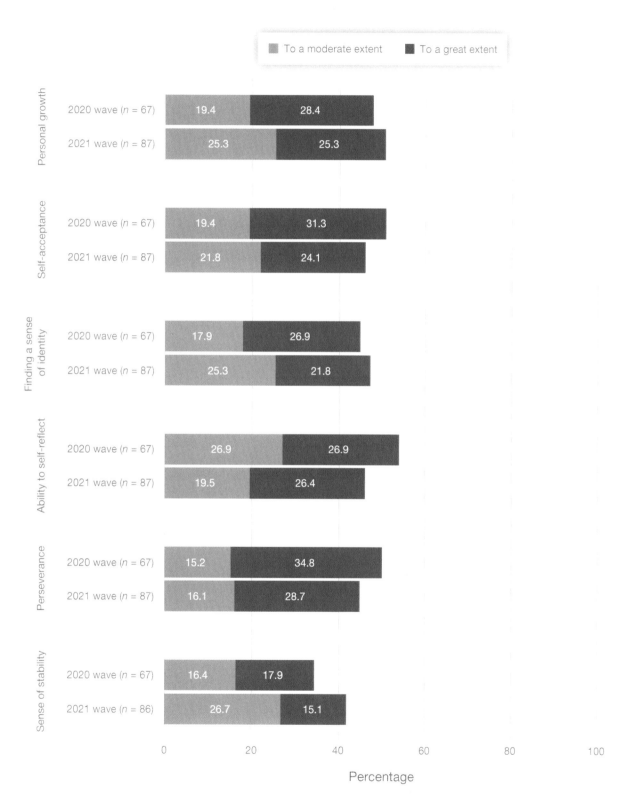

ship continues to contribute to their personal growth, self-acceptance, finding a sense of identity, ability to self-reflect, and perseverance, and this was consistent in both 2020 and 2021. A somewhat smaller percentage of respondents indicated that the fellowship continues to contribute to a sense of stability (34 percent in 2020, 41 percent in 2021). We conducted analyses with the subset of 44 individuals who responded to both surveys to see if there were any significant changes in their survey responses from 2020 to 2021, and found just one significant change. Specifically, individuals reported that the fellowship contributed more to their ability to self-reflect in 2020 than in 2021 ($p = 0.02$).[3] We also explored differences in responses between those who completed the fellowship fully in-person (the first seven cohorts) versus fully virtually (the most recent two cohorts), finding no significant differences (results not shown). This underscores the fact that the fellowship continues to have a meaningful effect on the lives of alumni.

Perceived Effect of Dog Tag Inc. on Professional Life and Personal Life

Respondents were also asked a series of items regarding the ways that the Dog Tag fellowship may have affected their personal and professional lives. For each statement, respondents selected their level of agreement on a five-point scale ranging from "strongly disagree" to "strongly agree." About three-quarters of respondents indicated that the fellowship continues to make a positive contribution to their professional and personal lives (see Figure 5.5). A substantial proportion of fellows also reported that the fellowship has helped them to take the next steps to pursue their personal goals and to clarify their professional goals, with especially high percentages in 2021 (87 and 86 percent, respectively).

In addition, more that 80 percent of respondents agreed that they feel more confident in the decisions they make about their professional life as a result of the fellowship, and more than 85 percent said that the fellowship had given them the tools they need to seek new professional opportunities (see Figure 5.6). Slightly fewer respondents said that the fellowship had helped them feel more excited about their professional prospects (about 70 percent in 2020 and 78 percent in 2021), though the majority agreed with these statements. Around 80 percent agreed that the fellowship helped them chart a path that builds on their strengths.

Similarly high proportions of respondents agreed that the fellowship helped them approach their professional life in a more flexible way and increased their access to new career paths, with slightly more respondents agreeing with these statements in 2021 than 2020 (Figure 5.7). At least 60 percent of respondents indicated that the fellowship helped them feel more comfortable working in nonmilitary settings or helped them feel like they have a professional mission.

Though there was some variation in responses across items and years, the responses to these statements suggest that the fellowship has affected several aspects of fellows' personal and professional lives, helping them to learn about different career paths, figure out how to leverage their strengths when looking for professional opportunities, and increasing their motivation and excitement to pursue various career paths. In fact, in 2020, 98.4 percent of respondents said that they agreed or strongly agreed with at least one of these 12 items, and 79.7 percent endorsed at least six of the 12 items; in 2021, 98.8 percent reported that they agreed or strongly agreed with at least one of these items, and 91.9 percent agreed with at least six of the 12 items. This suggests that it is not simply that each alumnus is able to find a single area of their life that has been affected by the fellowship; rather, alumni are reporting that several areas of their life have benefited from the fellowship experience.

As final analyses, we examined whether responses on these 12 items changed significantly from 2020 to 2021 among the 44 respondents who completed both surveys. We found no significant differences in ratings

---

[3]   To conduct the longitudinal analyses, we treated the five-point response scale as a continuous variable to allow us to conduct a repeated measures t-test. Mean in 2020 was 3.61 ($SD = 1.08$) and mean in 2021 was 3.16 ($SD = 1.33$), $t(43) = 2.49$.

FIGURE 5.5

Perceived Effect of Fellowship on Personal and Professional Life (Part 1)

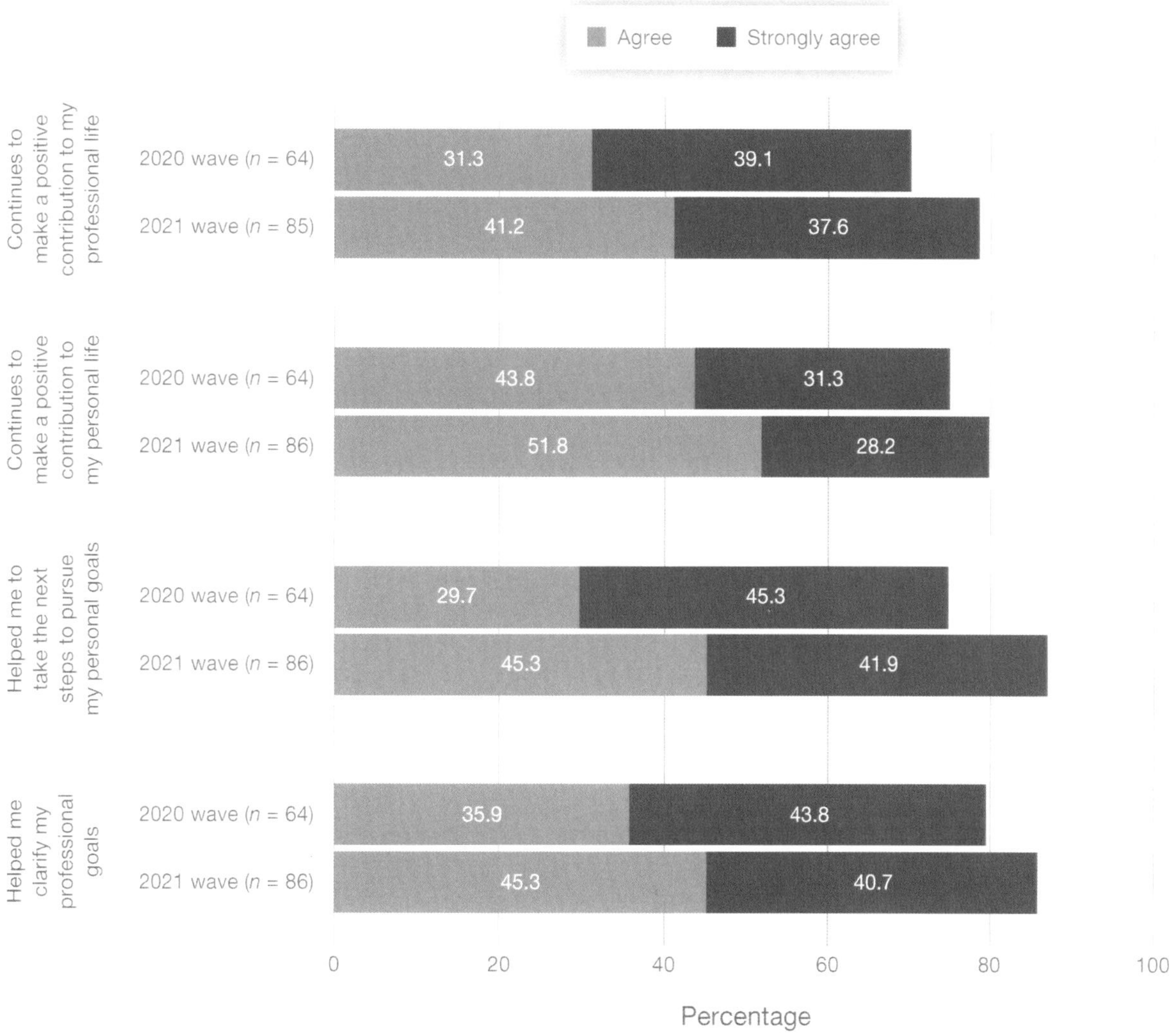

on each item between years (results not shown). We also explored differences in responses between those who completed the fellowship fully in-person versus fully virtually. The only significant difference was on the item "The Dog Tag Inc. Fellowship gave me the tools I needed to seek new professional opportunities" (chi square = 6.08, $df = 2$, $p = 0.047$). Those who completed the fellowship online had higher ratings on this item than those who completed it in-person, though this may reflect *when* the fellowship was completed rather than the format—that is, those who completed it more recently may be more likely to endorse this item than those who completed the fellowship more than two years ago.

Finally, in 2021 we added one item to assess whether the fellowship had provided respondents with tools, resources, or community connections that they used to get through the COVID-19 pandemic. In total, 67.5 percent of respondents agreed or strongly agreed with this statement (see Figure 5.8).

FIGURE 5.6

Perceived Effect of Fellowship on Personal and Professional Life (Part 2)

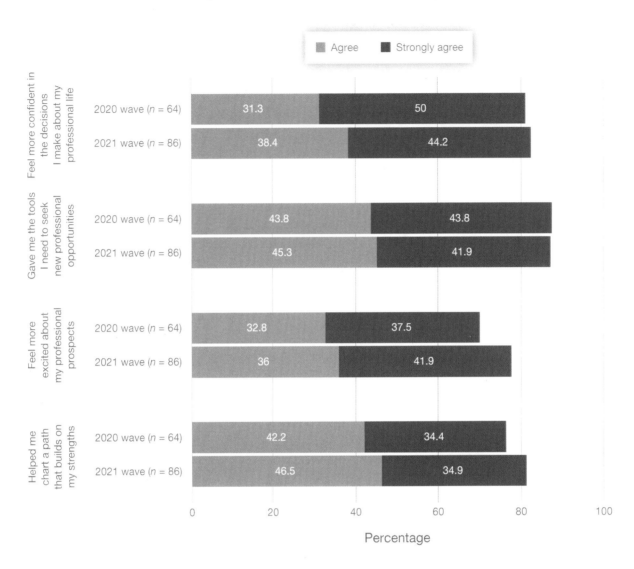

FIGURE 5.7

Perceived Effect of Fellowship on Personal and Professional Life (Part 3)

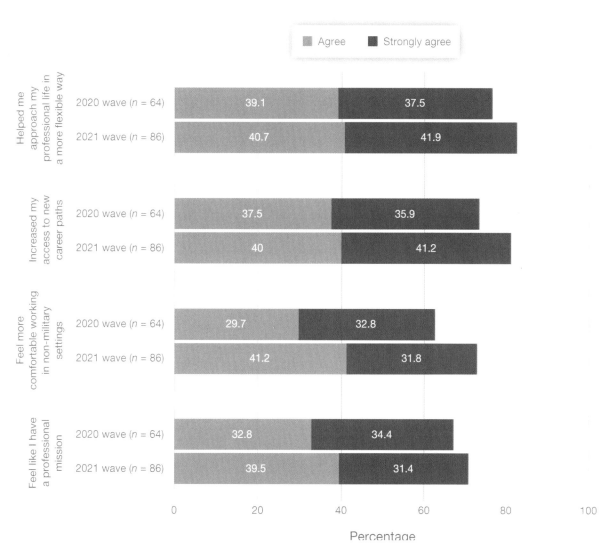

FIGURE 5.8

Percentage Reporting Fellowship Provided Resources to Navigate COVID-19

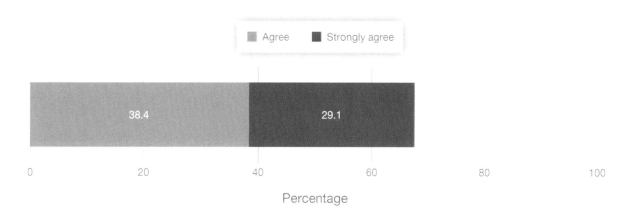

Enriched Life Scale

The items described in the previous section were designed to be explicitly related to the fellowship experience. In addition, we hypothesized there would be value in understanding how the experiences of alumni compared with other populations, including military and civilian populations. Therefore, we included three subscales from the Enriched Life Scale (Angel et al., 2020), a measure developed by personnel from Team Red, White & Blue, a veteran service organization, and validated in a sample of veterans and civilians. These subscales included Sense of Purpose, Genuine Relationships, and Engaged Citizenship. Responses to each item on each subscale were made on a five-point scale ranging from "strongly disagree" to "strongly agree." To compute each subscale score, responses to each item are standardized into a 0 to 100 scale and the mean of each item computed. Higher scores indicate a more positive experience (e.g., greater sense of purpose), and the scales had good internal consistency in this sample.[4] A global one-item question from this scale was also included. In Figure 5.9, we summarize the scores from survey respondents 2020 and 2021, as well as the mean score from the validation sample (Angel et al., 2020). Subscale scores were similar in both 2020 and 2021 across each of the subscales and the Global Enrichment Score; moreover, scores in our samples were very similar to that in the validation sample (Angel et al., 2020), suggesting that the experience of fellows may be similar to veterans and civilians reached by other veteran-serving organizations.

When we examined the 44 respondents who completed both surveys, there was no significant change on the Sense of Purpose or Engaged Citizenship subscales, nor on the Global Enrichment Score. However, mean scores on the Genuine Relationships subscale decreased from 82.54 ($SD = 14.26$) in 2020 to 78.20 ($SD = 16.01$) in 2021. It is possible that this may reflect the effect of the pandemic. However, we also found that individu-

FIGURE 5.9

Scores on the Enriched Life Scale

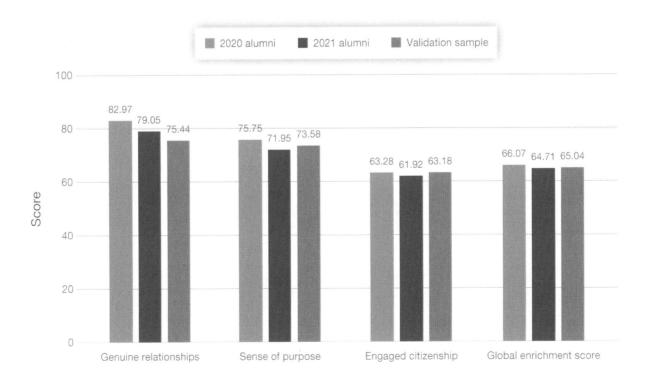

---

4   Cronbach's alpha for Genuine Relationships was 0.91 in 2020 and 0.96 in 2021; for Sense of Purpose was 0.94 in 2020 and 2021; and for Engaged Citizenship was 0.89 in 2020 and 0.90 in 2021.

als who completed the fellowship in a fully virtual format had a higher score on this subscale ($M = 80.61$) than those who completed the fellowship in-person ($M = 77.57$). This could reflect the passage of time (i.e., those who completed the fellowship more recently feel they have more genuine relationships than those who completed the program pre-pandemic), but without baseline data on this measure, this finding is difficult to interpret. There were no other differences based on fellowship format (virtual versus in-person).

Post-Fellowship Experiences

Pursuit of Additional Education

Fellows were asked whether they had pursued additional education since completing the fellowship. In 2020, about 56 percent of respondents said they had pursued education; among these 38 individuals, 24 indicated their decision was influenced by the fellowship (63 percent of the individuals pursuing education) (Figure 5.10). In 2021, the percentage of respondents reporting that they had pursued additional education had increased to 69 percent. Among these 60 alumni, 41 said that their decision to pursue education had been influenced by the fellowship (68 percent of the individuals pursuing education).

Civic Engagement

The DTI fellowship aims to promote participant engagement in their communities. Slightly more than half of respondents in both 2020 and 2021 indicated that they are engaged in work, education, or volunteering that serves their local community. In addition, 40 percent of respondents in 2020 and 45 percent in 2021 indicated that their work, education, or volunteering serves the larger community of veterans, their families, and/or caregivers (Figure 5.11).

Through the fellowship, alumni gain the skills to develop and work toward a business idea. In 2020, about half of the respondents indicated that they were currently working on a business idea (52 percent; $n = 34$); among those individuals, 18 said that they were working on the same business idea they were working on as a fellow (53 percent of the respondents who were working on a business plan) (see Figure 5.12). In 2021, these numbers increased slightly—about 58 percent of respondents were working on a business idea ($n = 50$). Among those, about 58 percent ($n = 29$) were working on the same business idea they were working on as a fellow. We conducted an analysis to determine whether there were any differences in the percentage of fellows

FIGURE 5.10

Percentage of Fellows Pursuing Additional Education Since Fellowship

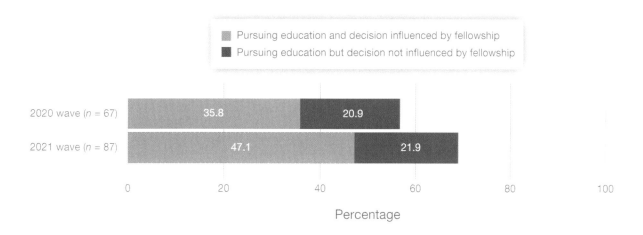

FIGURE 5.11
Community Engagement

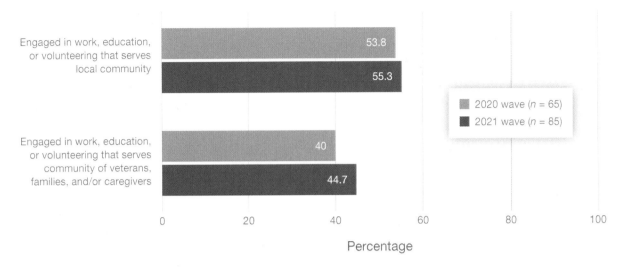

FIGURE 5.12
Percentage of Fellows Working on a Business Idea

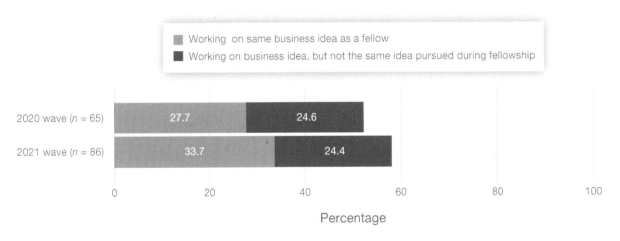

working on a business idea based on whether they attended fully in-person or fully virtual programming, and found no significant difference (chi square = 0.35, df = 1, p = 0.55). Similarly, there was no significant difference in the percentage reporting that it was the business idea they began working on as a fellow (chi square = 0.59, df = 1, p = 0.44).

We also examined how many respondents who reported working on a business idea also self-identified as entrepreneurs. For this analysis, we focused on the 2021 survey wave, as this was the wave in which we more explicitly asked respondents whether they were entrepreneurs. Of the 50 people who said they were working on a business idea in 2021, 46 percent (n = 23) identified as an entrepreneur.

Post-Fellowship Supports Learned About Through Dog Tag Inc.

In addition to the services provided directly by DTI, the program aims to connect fellows with other supports that they can access after completion of the fellowship. In both 2020 and 2021, the most common type of support reported by fellows was ongoing contact with DTI (Table 5.5). The next most common support in 2020 was fellowship or training programs offered by other veteran serving organizations, which included Bunker Labs, Elizabeth Dole Foundation, Blue Star Families, the Institute for Veterans and Military Families, and Wounded Warrior Project (WWP). By the 2021 survey, DTI had established a more formal relationship with WWP, and it had become the second most common support that respondents learned about through DTI. Less than 10 percent of respondents participated in fellowship or training programs offered through non-veteran-serving organizations, which included the Florida State University Jim Morgan Institute and the Bank of America Institute for Women's Entrepreneurship.

TABLE 5.5

Post-Fellowship Supports Learned About Through Dog Tag Inc.

Type of Support[a]	2020 Wave (N = 67) % (n)	2021 Wave (N = 87) % (n)
Fellowship or training program through VSO[b]	22.4% (15)	25.3% (22)
Fellowship or training program, not through VSO[c]	9.0% (6)	8.0% (7)
Ongoing contact with DTI	68.7% (46)	73.6% (64)
Wounded Warrior Project	–	36.8% (32)
None of the above	22.4% (15)	18.4% (16)

NOTE: VSO = veteran service organization.

[a] Item was "check all that apply," so categories do not necessarily add up to 100%.

[b] Responses included Bunker Labs, WWP, Elizabeth Dole Foundation, Rosie Network, The Military Coalition, HillVets, Syracuse University Veterans Program for Politics, Blue Star Families, Institute for Veterans and Military Families, Operation Gratitude, Steven Cohen Easter Seals, Entrepreneurship Bootcamp for Veterans, Pillars of Strength, Vets in Tech, 100 Entrepreneurs Project, Mayor's Office of Veterans Affairs, Capitol Post, Armed to Farm, SealFit, Mighty Oaks, Hiring our Heroes, Veteran in Residence.

[c] Responses included Give an Hour, Summit Fellowship, Bank of America Institute for Women's Entrepreneurship, The Paradigm Switch, Entnest, Florida State University Jim Morgan Institute, certain colleges and universities, Future Harvest.

Alumni Engagement

As noted, many former fellows receive ongoing support from DTI after completing their fellowship. We asked fellows what alumni activities they participated in during the past 12 months. In 2020, the most common activities were social gatherings and networking (45 percent), receiving personal support from DTI staff or board members (31 percent), and engagement with fellows during orientation and graduation weeks (26 percent) (Figure 5.13). In total, 68.8 percent of respondents reported participating in one or more of the pre-specified alumni activities (excluding responses to the "other" category), and the mean number of activities was 1.88 (SD = 1.94).

In 2021, in collaboration with DTI, we revised the response options for this item to better reflect their current alumni activity offerings. In 2021, the most common alumni activities among respondents were alumni check-in calls and social events (57 percent), engagement with fellows during orientation and graduation weeks (30 percent), and the DTI mentorship program (29 percent) (Figure 5.14). In total, 72.1 percent of respondents reported participating in one or more of the pre-specified alumni activities (excluding responses to the "other" category), and the mean number of activities was 2.12 (SD = 2.12).

FIGURE 5.13
Alumni Engagement Based on 2020 Survey

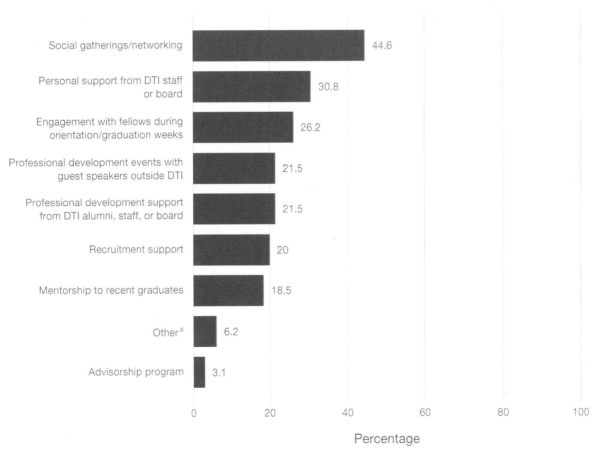

NOTE: Item was "check all that apply," so categories do not necessarily add up to 100%.
[a] Other responses included informal connections, alumni calls and interviews, election day.

FIGURE 5.14

Alumni Engagement Based on 2021 Survey

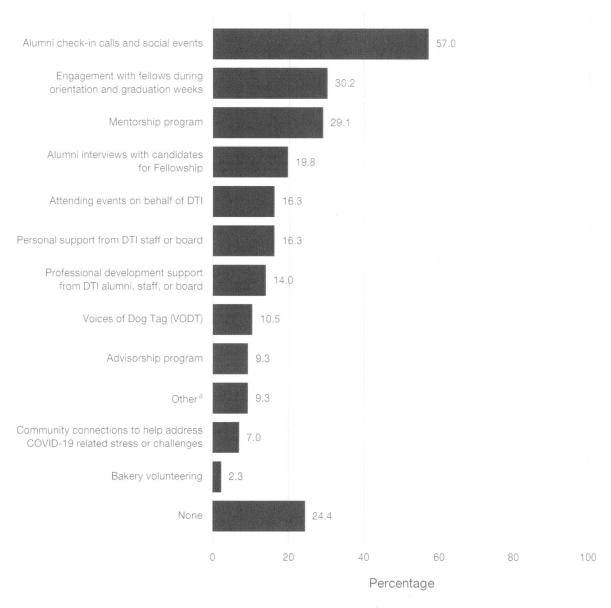

NOTE: Item was "check all that apply," so categories do not necessarily add up to 100%.

[a] Other responses included sharing the work about DTI to the military community (spouses, warriors, etc.); personal growth and friendship with alumni; partnerships with other nonprofits; volunteering for other alumni projects; "love by the DTI familia"; project advising.

Post-Fellowship Pursuit of Goals

Current Focus and Priorities

DTI understands that fellows have a range of priorities after they leave the fellowship, with some investing time in professional pursuits and others prioritizing their personal life and well-being. In 2020, we asked fellows to rank their primary focus, with options including personal well-being, career/employment, education, and "other." It was optional for participants to specify an "other" priority; if they did specify something in this category, they ranked the items 1 to 4, with 1 as the most important priority. If they did not, they ranked the three pre-specified options (personal well-being, career/employment, education) from 1 to 3. Results indicated that the most common first-place priority was personal well-being, followed by career/employment, then education, and then other (which included priorities such as family, financial well-being, and health) (Figure 5.15). Personal well-being was also the most common second-place priority, followed by career/employment, education, and other.

This question was asked again in 2021, with an additional option added: COVID-19-related challenges. As with 2020, the most common first-place priority was personal well-being, followed by career/employment, education, and "other" (including family, personal life changes, and travel) (Figure 5.16). Very few people ranked COVID-19-related challenges as their primary focus. However, unlike 2020, the most common second-place priority was education, followed by personal well-being and career/employment. This mirrors the trend reported earlier, with more fellows seeking postsecondary education or training in 2021 than 2020. As we gain further distance from the onset of the pandemic, it will be interesting to see if this is part of a larger trend for people to retrain or seek additional education as they prepare for different career paths.

FIGURE 5.15

Current Focus Based on 2020 Survey

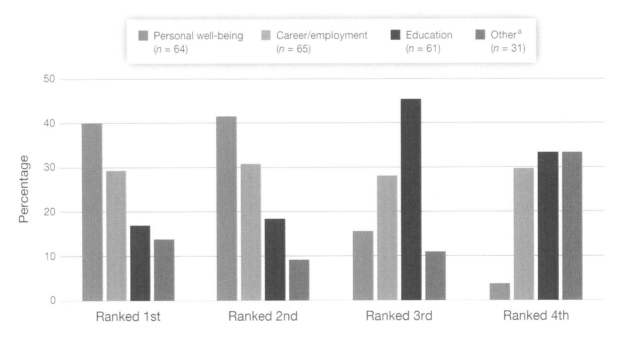

NOTE: N = 65.

[a] Other responses included family, financial well-being, COVID-19 pandemic, health, service, and other personal and professional goals.

FIGURE 5.16

Current Focus Based on 2021 Survey

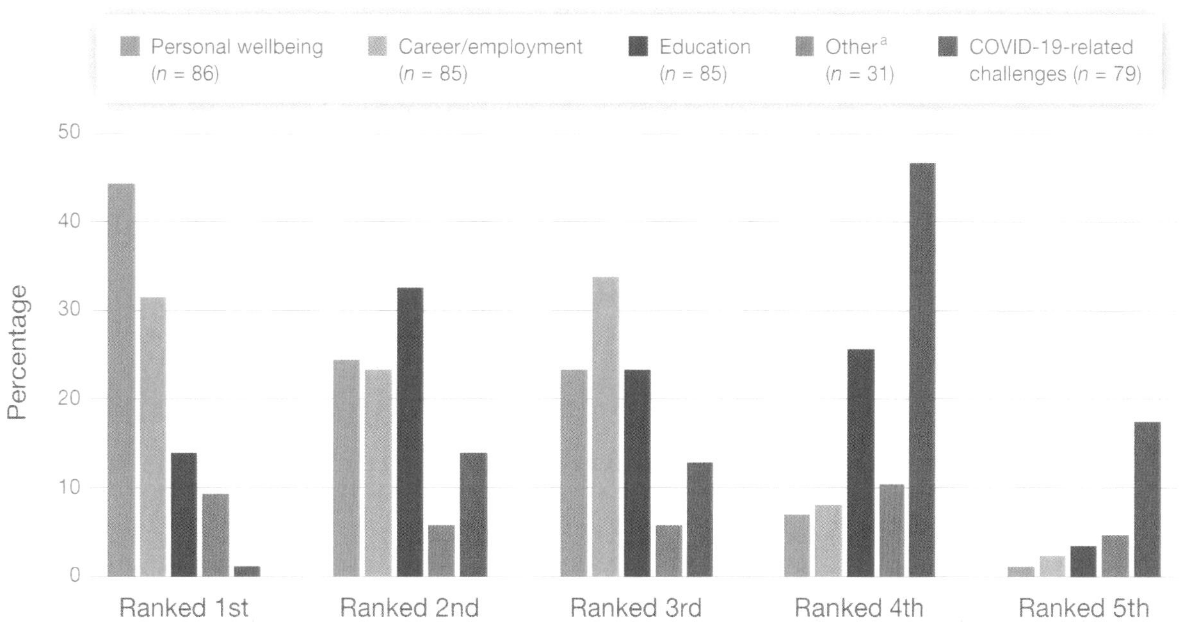

NOTE: *N* = 86.

ª Other responses included family, VA claims, health, personal life changes (e.g., wedding, moving), travel, and spirituality.

Challenges to Pursuing Goals

During the qualitative interviews, fellows highlighted a number of challenges they encountered to pursuing their goals, including both personal and professional goals. Based on their responses and the literature on reintegration among veterans, spouses, and caregivers, we asked respondents to indicate the challenges they had experienced to pursuing their goals since completing the fellowship. In 2020, we asked about 14 specific challenges, and respondents could also write in other challenges they faced; in 2021, we added one additional option to indicate COVID-19-related challenges.

In both 2020 and 2021, the respondents' own physical or behavioral health conditions were the most commonly endorsed challenge, with about 50 percent of respondents indicating that this had been a challenge (Figure 5.17). The second most common challenge in both years was managing family needs. Interestingly, in 2020, changing geographic locations and disruptions in work history were endorsed as a challenge by about 30 percent of respondents; however, this percentage dropped to 21 percent in 2021. One possibility is that responses in 2020 reflected initial upheaval in living and employment situations due to the effect of COVID-19, but by fall 2021, that was less of a concern. By contrast, challenges maintaining connections with people was reported as a concern by more respondents in 2021 (36 percent) than 2020 (25 percent), which may reflect the effect that COVID-19 has had on feelings of connectedness and loneliness (Horigian, Schmidt, and Feaster, 2021).

In 2020, the average number of challenges selected by respondents was 3.53 (SD = 2.30; median = 3); in 2021, it was 3.78 (SD = 2.86; median = 3). Together, these findings underscore the wide range of challenges that this population encounters when pursuing their goals, even after completion of the fellowship.

DTI staff were interested in exploring how many people who reported that they were having challenges maintaining connections with people also participated in DTI alumni activities. In Table 5.6, we summarize the number who did and did not report difficulty maintaining connections each year; among those, we

FIGURE 5.17

Challenges to Pursuing Goals

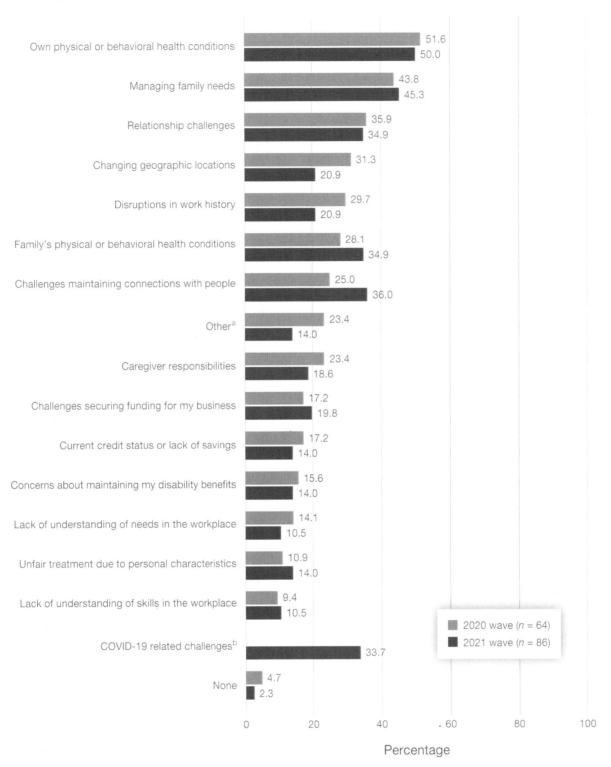

NOTE: Item was "check all that apply," so categories do not necessarily add up to 100%.

[a] Other responses included need more financial resources; toxic work environment; need additional education; divorcing service member and now disconnected from the supportive military community; gaining access to DoD and VA benefits; lost medical insurance coverage; transitioning out of military (spouse, self); transportation; opportunities in the geographic location are limited.

[b] Question new to the 2021 survey.

TABLE 5.6

Association Between Difficulty Maintaining Connections and Alumni Engagement

	2020		2021	
	Difficulty Maintaining Connections (*n* = 16)	No Difficulty Maintaining Connections (*n* = 48)	Difficulty Maintaining Connections (*n* = 31)	No Difficulty Maintaining Connections (*n* = 55)
Number reporting they did not participate in alumni activities (*n*, %)	3 (18.6%)	14 (29.2%)	5 (16.2%)	17 (30.9%)
Number participating in alumni activities (*n*, %)	13 (81.3%)	34 (70.8%)	26 (83.9%)	38 (69.0%)
Number of alumni activities reported (*M* (*SD*))	2.08 (1.12)	2.88 (1.93)	2.96 (1.34)	2.95 (2.36)

report what percentage did *not* participate in alumni activities; what percentage *did* participate; and, among those who participated, the mean number of activities they participated in (we counted "other" as a single activity for purposes of computing this mean). As shown in this table, most individuals who reported difficulty maintaining connections had participated in alumni activities (81 percent in 2020 and 84 percent in 2021)—and in fact, a greater percentage of individuals who had difficulty maintaining connections participated in alumni activities than those who did *not* have difficulty maintaining connections. This could reflect attempts on the part of these individuals to establish connections or leverage an existing support network.

Overall Satisfaction

Most of the items on the 2020 and 2021 survey changed too substantially to compare them to the prior survey waves in 2018 and 2019 (only three items had identical wording for both the questions and response option). However, we retained the original wording of an item assessing overall satisfaction. In the original three survey waves, responses were made on a seven-point scale (extremely dissatisfied, moderately dissatisfied, slightly dissatisfied, neither satisfied nor dissatisfied, slightly satisfied, moderately satisfied, and extremely satisfied). To reduce cognitive burden when responding to this item, we simplified the response options to a five-point scale in 2020 and 2021 (extremely dissatisfied, dissatisfied, neither satisfied nor dissatisfied, satisfied, and extremely satisfied). To compare across the five waves, we collapsed "moderately dissatisfied" and "slightly dissatisfied" into a single "dissatisfied" category, and "slightly satisfied" and "moderately satisfied" into a single "satisfied category."

Across the five waves of the survey, overall satisfaction remained quite high (Figure 5.18). More than 70 percent of respondents at each wave reported that they were extremely satisfied with the fellowship, and at least 94 percent reported that they were satisfied or extremely satisfied. Among the 44 respondents who participated in both survey waves, there was no significant change with time (results not shown). There were also no differences in ratings between those who completed the fellowship fully in-person and those who completed it in a fully virtual format.

In addition, we asked fellows to indicate, on a scale of 0 to 10, how likely they were to recommend this fellowship to a friend. The mean response in 2020 was 9.34 (*SD* = 1.48), and in 2021 was 9.45 (*SD* = 1.40). Taken together, these findings highlight the high levels of satisfaction among respondents.

FIGURE 5.18
Overall Satisfaction with the Dog Tag Inc. Fellowship

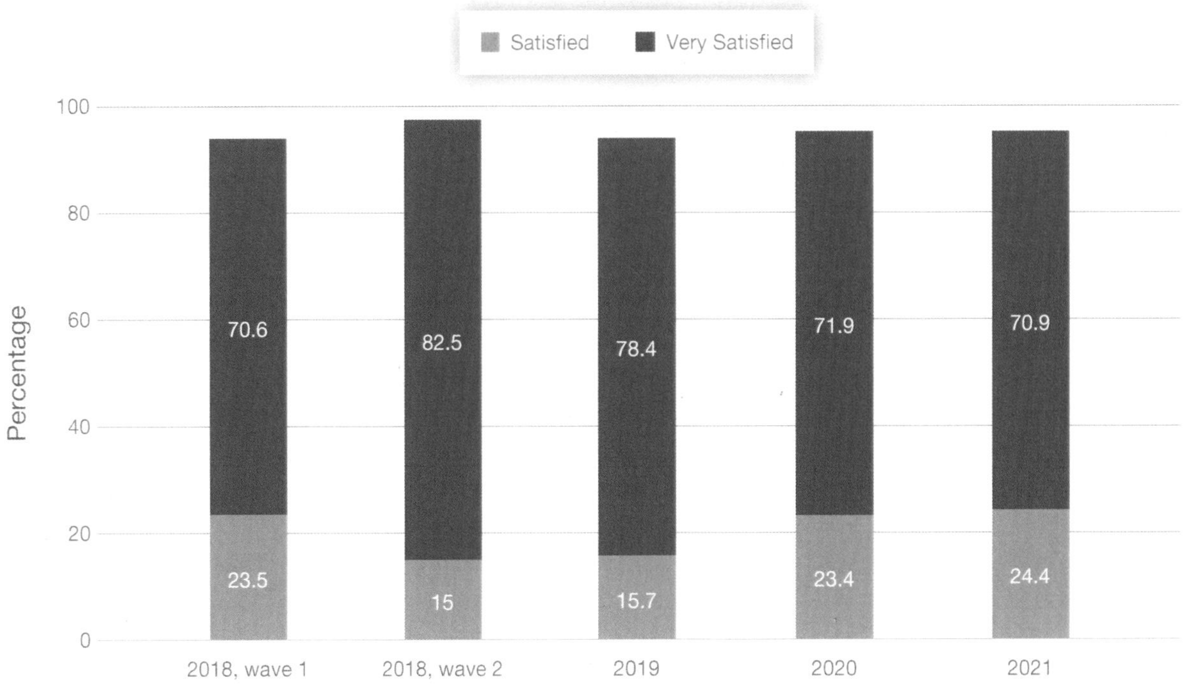

Conclusion

This chapter presented the results of the first two waves of the revised alumni survey. There are several strengths of our survey administration, including that over 50 percent of alumni respond to each survey and that the respondents included alumni from across all cohorts.

Most of our survey respondents were employed at least part-time. It was most common to be employed as a paid employee of a company, but some alumni were pursuing entrepreneurial pathways, often while they were employed in other positions or pursuing education. Interestingly, in 2021, substantially more fellows were pursuing postsecondary education. In the first year of the survey, nearly half of respondents reported that they were underemployed, though that number had dropped to about 30 percent in 2021, which may reflect some of the larger impact in the first year of COVID-19 on the job market.

The fellowship aims to help fellows find a pathway to a meaningful career or educational experience as they pursue their goals. We found that alumni had largely positive perceptions of their jobs and educational experiences, including overall satisfaction, and reported finding their experiences fulfilling, feeling comfortable advocating for themselves, and being satisfied with their work/life or school/life balance.

With this new survey, we asked more explicitly about the ongoing impact of the fellowship on areas such as personal growth, self-acceptance, and finding a sense of identity. For most items in both years, we found that more than 40 percent of respondents reported that the fellowship continued to affect these areas to a moderate or a great extent. This is impressive, especially given that some cohorts completed the fellowship several years ago, and we found no difference in responses between the most recent two cohorts and earlier cohorts. Similarly, responses highlighted the myriad ways that the fellowship has affected the personal and professional lives of fellows, including helping them to take the next steps to pursue their personal goals, helping them to clarify their professional goals, giving them the tools needed to pursue new professional opportunities, and helping them approach their professional life in a more flexible way.

Though we asked several questions specific to the alumnus's experience with the fellowship, we also included three subscales from the Enriched Life Scales, a validated scale developed by a veteran-serving organization. Overall, scores on this measure were high and very similar to those reported in the validation sample, suggesting that DTI alumni have similar experiences to those engaged with other veteran service organizations (VSOs).

Since completing the fellowship, an increasing number of fellows have pursued additional education or training, and about half have served their communities through their work, education, or volunteering. Many are working on their business idea—with about half of those working on the idea they began as a fellow. Several fellows have gone on to participate in other programs that they learned about through DTI, especially those offered by VSOs and the WWP. Fellows continue to stay engaged through the alumni programming. Social gatherings and events were among the most common alumni activities in both years of the survey. In 2020, personal support from DTI staff was also especially common.

Responses to the survey highlight that, although career, employment, and education are important to alumni, their primary focus is on their personal well-being. At the same time, alumni continue to encounter challenges to pursuing their goals, including their physical or behavioral health conditions, family needs, relationship challenges, and difficulty maintaining connections with other people.

Overall, survey responses highlight the high levels of satisfaction that fellows have with their fellowship experience. More than 94 percent of fellows reported that they are satisfied or very satisfied with the program, and fellows reported being extremely likely to recommend the fellowship to a friend.

CHAPTER SIX

Conclusion

We set out to elucidate the professional and personal impact of the DTI fellowship and to provide DTI with a tool, in the form of a revised survey, to better assess how the more than 100 fellows (a growing number) who have participated in the fellowship perceive the longitudinal impacts of their participation. We based the tool off of extensive qualitative, exploratory research to understand how alumni describe the program's impact in their own words. Then, we fielded two waves of the survey over two years to assess the longitudinal employment and general well-being outcomes of DTI alumni.

To understand the impact of DTI, one has to acknowledge the underlying challenges and the precariousness of transitions for U.S. veterans, military spouses, and military caregivers. As the literature review demonstrated, and the fellows corroborated, these challenges include substantial physical and mental health issues, traumatic experiences that are both combat-related and longstanding from childhood, issues with acculturation to civilian life, struggles with a sense of self-identity, and the difficulties inherent in relocation and starting anew.

The focus groups and interviews among nearly half of DTI's alumni largely reflect DTI's mission to help U.S. veterans who face service-connected disabilities, military spouses, and military caregivers "build resilience, find renewed purpose, and forge community beyond the military" (Dog Tag Inc., undated-b). Every fellow described the program as transformative personally, professionally, or both. In addition, fellows offered constructive feedback on components of the curriculum and other aspects of the program (summarized below). Although the revised survey strives to reflect several of the rich themes identified in the qualitative data, a survey cannot readily capture nuance and the transformative power of storytelling. For example, it is difficult to place a statistic on the several cases of fellows who poignantly stated that the program saved their lives. In that vein, it might be worth continuing to perform focus groups and interviews by a neutral third party at regular intervals (e.g., every two years) among a subsample of alumni to complement the survey data and gain a more in-depth understanding of the effects of each component of the fellowship.

The survey data provide insight into the post-fellowship experience of alumni, as well as the ways that the fellowship continues to influence the lives of fellows. Survey responses were consistent with many of the themes highlighted by the qualitative data, with 40 to 50 percent of respondents noting that the fellowship continues to contribute to their personal growth, self-acceptance, efforts to find a sense of identity, perseverance, and ability to self-reflect. On the most recent survey, about half also reported that the fellowship has contributed to a sense of stability in their lives. Responses to the survey also underscored many themes that we heard through the qualitative interviews—that the fellowship continues to affect their personal and professional life, including helping them pursue their personal goals, clarifying their professional goals, and giving them the foundation needed to seek new opportunities and chart a new course. Although the fellowship centers on building entrepreneurial opportunities through a holistic mind, body, educational program, some respondents noted that physical and behavioral issues can sometimes get in the way of pursuing their goals, as can family obligations. And though many alumni go on to serve their community, work toward a business plan, and pursue additional education, personal well-being remains a top priority. That said, many fellows remain connected to the fellowship as a source of support, with respondents reporting that they had participated in two to three alumni activities, on average, in the past year.

One notable aspect of this study is that it reflects DTI's commitment to systematically tracking the impacts of the fellowship on current fellows and alumni. As noted in the literature review, the important step of rigorously collecting data is rare among the nation's thousands of veteran support programs and services, and it should be considered a core strength of DTI. The revised alumni survey will continue to provide a quantitative perspective on the impacts of the program. In addition, the inclusion of the Enriched Life Scale (Angel et al., 2020) allows for comparisons with other veteran and civilian populations.

At the same time, there are also limitations to this analysis. The qualitative data were collected prior to the COVID-19 pandemic and may not reflect some of the experiences of the newer cohorts, particularly those who completed a fully virtual version of the fellowship. Another limitation is that the fellows who opted to participate in the interviews, focus groups, and surveys may have had different experiences from those who did not. For example, they may have had more favorable perceptions of DTI than those who did not. That said, for the interviews, we deliberately sampled individuals who had been less engaged with the fellowship to gain a range of opinions, and interviewees were made aware that DTI staff would not be told about their participation, so as to reduce a social desirability bias. For the survey, offering an incentive and having a third party host the survey in a confidential manner—rather than DTI being the survey host and being able to connect individuals to their responses—may also have increased the chances that individuals with a range of perceptions participated. In addition, data collection occurred during the pandemic, which has had a substantial impact on the labor market, and it is difficult to know whether the findings would be consistent with fellow experiences pre-pandemic. Finally, there was a small subsample that participated in both waves of the survey, limiting our ability to detect significant change over time. The fairly small sample also limited our ability to perform other subgroup analyses.

Though this survey was not fielded as part of a formal program evaluation, it is also important to consider additional limits to the conclusions of this study. For example, we focused only on a snapshot in time of the alumni experience. Because we did not have pre-fellowship data, or even data from the window immediately post-fellowship, it is difficult to know whether or how the fellowship contributed to changes on some of the constructs measured by the alumni survey. For example, administering the Enriched Life Scale at the beginning of the fellowship, at the end of the fellowship, and through the alumni survey would allow us to examine change over time. An even more rigorous approach to evaluating the program would be to measure these outcomes among a comparison group of individuals who did not participate in the fellowship, as we cannot determine whether the DTI program or other external factors led to the observed results. In addition, it is important to keep in mind that this project was designed to be specific to the Dog Tag Inc. fellowship, which means that the findings may not generalize to the broader population of U.S. veterans, caregivers, and spouses who are undergoing the transition to civilian life; in other words, we do not know whether the DTI fellows are representative of the broader population of post-9/11 veterans, caregivers, and spouses.

Recommendations

The DTI Fellowship fills an important need for veterans, spouses, and caregivers. Research has shown that employment is a key service need for service members as they transition to the civilian community (Perkins et al., 2022; Derefinko et al., 2019). There is also evidence that veterans may be especially open to pursuing entrepreneurial pathways; for example, veterans are more likely to be self-employed (Heinz et al., 2017), and an evaluation of one entrepreneurship training program found that military participants had a higher percentage of business launches than civilian participants (Kerrick, Cumberland, and Choi, 2016).

Regarding spouses and caregivers, military spouses have been shown to work fewer hours and make less money than their civilian counterparts (Meadows et al., 2015; Keeling et al., 2020), but there is also less research about employment-related needs of these groups, though the military-to-civilian transition also affects their personal and professional lives (Keeling et al., 2020; Bommarito et al., 2017).

By enrolling veterans, spouses, and caregivers, DTI is potentially reaching a larger population of individuals in need. And addressing employment goals has important implications, with the potential to produce gains in areas ranging from earning to resilience to mental and physical health (Bond et al., 2021; Heinz et al., 2017). Moreover, by formally integrating programming related to wellness and reflection, DTI is also creating a space for fellows to simultaneously address their personal goals and well-being. The demand for and success of the program is additionally demonstrated by DTI's recent expansion to a second site, based in Chicago.

As an organization, DTI is continuously evaluating and revising its program model to ensure that it is meeting the needs of its fellows. Our findings suggest that the program is successful in its efforts to support fellows in the pursuit of professional and personal opportunities. However, based on the findings from this study, we propose the following recommendations for DTI to consider as the organization continues to fine-tune, expand, and evaluate its program:

- **Continue to monitor the ways that the COVID-19 pandemic has affected the employment sector, including its effect on entrepreneurship.** Alumni survey data suggest that the COVID-19 pandemic may have affected alumni's employment, such as creating a period of underemployment or spurring alumni to pursue additional education. Though, as of mid-2022, the employment market has stabilized to some degree, many individuals remain out of work, and certain groups are especially affected (e.g., employees in lower-wage industries, women, marginalized racial and ethnic groups) (Kocchar and Bennett, 2021; Center on Budget and Policy Priorities, 2021). The fellowship will be especially relevant if it can explicitly address these topics in its curriculum (e.g., how to navigate entrepreneurial pursuits during times of potentially heightened financially instability).

- **Determine what role DTI wants to play in supporting alumni, and consider offering programming, resources, or awareness building efforts to address common alumni challenges.** DTI has expanded its alumni offerings and now has a robust range of offerings available to alumni. Based on the survey, many alumni are willing to engage in this alumni programming. At the same time, survey respondents identified a number of ongoing challenges that they continue to face. Although there are certain domains that are outside the scope of what DTI can address through its alumni programs (e.g., unfair treatment in the workplace, behavioral health challenges), resources could be provided to help to address challenges such as impediments to securing funding or a lack of understanding about the needs of veterans, spouses, and caregivers in the workplace. In this way, DTI could use findings from this survey to identify additional ways to support alumni.

- **Consider the role of technology in the program for future cohorts.** The current state of the pandemic has made it possible for more workplaces to return to in-person operations. Being on-site can have advantages in terms of team building, leadership development, and other complex tasks (Ringel, 2021). At the same time, there are also advantages to virtual programming, especially for fellows who may have family obligations or caregiving responsibilities (Van Bommel, 2021), or find it difficult to relocate to one of the Dog Tag Inc. sites. Our findings suggest that individuals who completed a fully virtual fellowship had equally positive ratings of the impact of the fellowship as previous cohorts, though it is also important to keep in mind that this might also reflect that these were also the most recent two cohorts, and the recency of their experiences or pandemic-related considerations may have contributed to their ratings.

- **Identify ways to maintain fidelity to the DTI model as the program grows.** As the DTI fellowship expands, program staff will face the challenge of replicating the most effective components of the program, while also taking into account any unique features of the new Chicago site. The program already has a well-established program model and theory of change, which will help support implementation at this new site. An additional practice that DTI may consider is a program "champion." The champion concept originates in implementation science and refers to a person who goes above and beyond their role to influence the success of the program. This person can support and promote the program, as well as address barriers or resistance (Powell et al., 2015). However, as noted previously, it can be difficult to hire individuals with the kinds of intangible characteristics known to make a successful program champion—characteristics such as persuasiveness, grit, and a participative leadership style (Bonawitz et al., 2020). Whether DTI is able to find an existing staff member who can serve this type of role for their new site, or whether the organization hires someone externally who contributes these characteristics, having a program champion may increase the success of DTI's new Chicago site.

- **Find opportunities to diversify the staff of the organization and ensure their cultural competence with military populations.** During qualitative interviews, some fellows noted that increasing the diversity of the organization would be beneficial—particularly with respect to leadership positions and composition of the board. This could include diversity with respect to gender and race. Others noted that it is important to ensure that staff are attuned to the unique needs of military populations to ensure the comfort of all fellows.

- **Continue administering the annual alumni survey, and continue to bolster data collection at enrollment and completion of the program in a way that complements the alumni survey.** Now that the survey has been fielded twice and refined, an annual survey represents a low-cost way for the fellowship to continue monitoring the post-fellowship experiences of alumni. We recommend continuing to administer the survey on an annual basis. In addition, in our initial work to revise the DTI alumni survey, we provided recommendations to the organization about ways that it could add corresponding questions upon enrollment to the program (e.g., through the application or a baseline survey) and upon completion of the program. This would allow DTI to track trends over time with respect to key indicators, such as the Enriched Life Scale subscales.

- **Perform regular focus groups and interviews, facilitated by a third party.** Though the survey provides a straightforward, efficient way to reach all alumni at once, it is not possible for a quantitative survey to capture the rich nuance that emerged from our focus groups and interviews with fellows and alumni. We believe there is value in continuing to collect qualitative data, especially as it might reveal additional benefits of the programs or elucidate ways in which the program may improve upon its current offerings, beyond what the survey is able to capture. We recommend a third party facilitate these focus groups or interviews because it will help to avoid any social desirability bias on the part of participants (i.e., the potential for fellows to provide largely positive feedback because they are talking to program staff with whom they already have a relationship).

- **Explore the possibility of conducting a formal evaluation of the DTI fellowship.** The alumni survey is an important aspect of detecting the longer-term outcomes that fellows achieve. However, it can be difficult to know what outcomes were observed as a result of the fellowship versus other external factors, even when questions ask about the influence of the fellowship. As the fellowship grows, DTI may be interested in more formally evaluating the program, including a process evaluation, which focuses on program implementation, and an outcome evaluation, which would require a more coordinated data collection process (e.g., adding pre-fellowship and immediate post-fellowship data collection as suggested above) and potentially the identification of a comparison group. This type of evaluation could help to further develop the evidence base for the DTI model.

Apart from these program-specific recommendations, this study—and the broader literature—highlight the importance of providing support to veterans, caregivers, and spouses as they navigate the transition to civilian life. Rigorous data collection and analyses will be increasingly important as more veterans separate from military service. Tracking employment opportunities and related social, health, and well-being outcomes over time will also help identify differential outcomes among veterans, caregivers, and spouses.

Conclusion

In conclusion, alumni of the DTI fellowship recounted several ways in which the program affected their personal and professional trajectories. The careful attention given to systematically and rigorously tracking how this impact unfolds over time and how to continuously improve the program is valuable, and the nation's veterans, military families, and military caregivers deserve nothing short of these tools to foster successful reintegration. As service members and their families continue to transition to post-military civilian life, veteran service organizations and the American public alike can benefit from understanding the impacts of programs such as Dog Tag Inc. and the opportunities that veterans, spouses, and caregivers bring to communities, labor markets, and the nation.

Revised Survey

In this appendix, we present the alumni survey fielded by RAND in 2020 and 2021. As described in Appendix B, this version of the survey was developed by RAND in partnership with DTI and was revised from a previous version of the alumni survey fielded in 2018 and 2019. In Table A.1, we present each survey item and indicate the source of each item (e.g., whether the item was taken or adapted from the original alumni survey, developed specifically for purposes of this survey, or taken from a validated survey). In addition, there were slight changes from the version fielded in 2020 and 2021, and these are indicated in Table A.1.

TABLE A.1

Dog Tag Inc. Alumni Survey

Survey Item	Years Fielded	Sources
How much has your **personal** life changed as a result of the COVID-19 outbreak? • Stayed about the same • Changed, but only a little bit • Changed in a major way	2020	Adapted from Pew Research Center, 2020
How much has your **professional** life changed as a result of the COVID-19 outbreak? • Stayed about the same • Changed, but only a little bit • Changed in a major way	2020	Adapted from Pew Research Center, 2020
Which of the following describe your current employment status? Mark all that apply. • Full-Time Employed (32 or more hours per week), non-self-employment • Full-Time Employed (32 or more hours per week), self-employed • Part-Time Employed (fewer than 32 hours per week), non-self-employment • Part-Time Employed (fewer than 32 hours per week), self-employed • Unemployed • Volunteer • In Full-Time Post-Secondary Education (including degree, certificate, or other training programs) • In Part-Time Post-Secondary Education (including degree, certificate, or other training programs) • In Military Transition (still active duty)	2020	Adapted from previous DTI alumni survey
(If respondent selects full-time or part-time employment) Please enter number of years at current place of employment, in years and months. _____ years, _____ months	2020	Adapted from previous DTI alumni survey

Table A.1—continued

Survey Item	Years Fielded	Sources
Which of the following describe your current employment status? Mark all that apply. • Full-Time Employed (paid employee working for a company 32 or more hours per week) • Part-Time Employed (paid employee working for a company less than 32 hours per week) • Full-Time Entrepreneur (32 or more hours per week) • Part-Time Entrepreneur (less than 32 hours per week) • Unemployed, by choice • Unemployed, seeking employment • Volunteer • In Full-Time Post-Secondary Education (including degree, certificate, or other training programs) • In Part-Time Post-Secondary Education (including degree, certificate, or other training programs) • In Military Transition (still active duty)	2021	Response options updated from 2020 survey item
(If respondent selects full-time or part-time employed) Please enter number of years at current place of employment in years and months. (For this question, focus on your role as a paid employee working for a company. If you also selected that you are an entrepreneur, you will be asked about that next.) _____ years, _____ months	2021	Item updated from 2020 survey
(If respondent selects that they are an entrepreneur) Please enter the number of years that you have been working as an entrepreneur. _____ years, _____ months	2021	Item updated from 2020 survey
Do you consider yourself underemployed? For example, this means that your job does not fully use your education or training, or that you are working less than you would prefer. • Yes • No • I'm not sure	2020, 2021	Payscale, undated-b
(If yes or not sure) Tell us more about your employment situation. (Check all that apply.) • My job does not fully use my education or training. • I am working part-time but want full-time work. • I am underemployed due to the effect of the COVID-19 pandemic. • Other (please specify) _____	2020, 2021 (note: third response option asked in 2021 only)	Adapted from Payscale, undated-b
Please indicate your marital status. • Single • Married • Living with partner • Other	2020, 2021	Previous DTI alumni survey
What is the highest level of education you have achieved? • High school • GED • Some college • Associate's degree • Bachelor's degree • Master's degree • PhD • Other	2020, 2021	Previous DTI alumni survey
Have you pursued additional education (e.g., degree, certificate, training program) since completing the Fellowship? • Yes • No	2020, 2021	Developed for current survey

Table A.1—continued

Survey Item	Years Fielded	Sources
(If Yes) Was your choice to pursue additional education influenced by your participation in the DTI Fellowship? • Yes • No	2020, 2021	Developed for current survey
Which category best describes your current **personal** income? • Less than $20,000 • $20,000–$35,000 • $35,001–$50,000 • $50,001–$75,000 • $75,001–$100,000 • $100,001–$150,000 • $150,001–$250,000 • More than $250,001 • Prefer not to answer	2020, 2021	Adapted from previous DTI alumni survey
Which category best describes your current **household** income? • Less than $20,000 • $20,000–$35,000 • $35,001–$50,000 • $50,001–$75,000 • $75,001–$100,000 • $100,001–$150,000 • $150,001–$250,000 • More than $250,001 • Prefer not to answer	2020, 2021	Adapted from previous DTI alumni survey
Since the end of the Fellowship, what sources of support have you used that you learned about through DTI? Check all that apply. • Fellowship or training programs offered through other veterans service organizations • Please specify: _____ • Fellowship or training programs offered through nonveteran-specific organizations • Please specify: _____ • Ongoing contact with Dog Tag Inc. • Wounded Warrior Project (WWP) resources or programming • None of the above	2020, 2021 (note: WWP response option asked in 2021 only)	Developed for current survey

[For currently employed Fellows]

Survey Item	Years Fielded	Sources
How satisfied or dissatisfied are you with your current job? • Extremely satisfied • Satisfied • Neither satisfied nor dissatisfied • Dissatisfied • Extremely dissatisfied	2020, 2021	Adapted from previous DTI alumni survey
How fulfilling is your work? • Extremely fulfilling • Fulfilling • Neither fulfilling nor unfulfilling • Unfulfilling • Extremely unfulfilling	2020, 2021	Adapted from previous DTI alumni survey
How comfortable are you advocating for your needs in your current employment experience (e.g., communicating with your supervisors, establishing boundaries with coworkers or clients)? • Extremely comfortable • Comfortable • Neither comfortable nor uncomfortable • Uncomfortable • Extremely uncomfortable	2020, 2021	Adapted from previous DTI alumni survey

Table A.1—continued

Survey Item	Years Fielded	Sources
How satisfied are you with your ability to maintain a healthy work/life balance? • Extremely satisfied • Satisfied • Neither satisfied nor dissatisfied • Dissatisfied • Extremely dissatisfied	2020, 2021	Developed for current survey
[For Fellows participating in a post-secondary educational program]		
How satisfied or dissatisfied are you with your current post-secondary education experience? • Extremely satisfied • Satisfied • Neither satisfied nor dissatisfied • Dissatisfied • Extremely dissatisfied	2020, 2021	Adapted from previous DTI alumni survey
How fulfilling is your current post-secondary education experience? • Extremely fulfilling • Fulfilling • Neither fulfilling nor unfulfilling • Unfulfilling • Extremely unfulfilling	2020, 2021	Adapted from previous DTI alumni survey
How comfortable are you advocating for your needs in your current post-secondary education experience (e.g., communicating with classmates and faculty)? • Extremely comfortable • Comfortable • Neither comfortable nor uncomfortable • Uncomfortable • Extremely uncomfortable	2020, 2021	Adapted from previous DTI alumni survey
How satisfied are you with your ability to maintain a healthy school/life balance? • Extremely satisfied • Satisfied • Neither satisfied nor dissatisfied • Dissatisfied • Extremely dissatisfied	2020, 2021	Developed for current survey
To what extent does the Dog Tag Inc. Fellowship currently *continue to contribute* to improvements in the following areas of your life?		
Personal growth. • Not at all • To a small extent • To some extent • To a moderate extent • To a great extent	2020, 2021	Developed for current survey
Self-acceptance. • Not at all • To a small extent • To some extent • To a moderate extent • To a great extent	2020, 2021	Developed for current survey
Finding a sense of identity. • Not at all • To a small extent • To some extent • To a moderate extent • To a great extent	2020, 2021	Developed for current survey

Table A.1—continued

Survey Item	Years Fielded	Sources
Ability to self-reflect. • Not at all • To a small extent • To some extent • To a moderate extent • To a great extent	2020, 2021	Developed for current survey
Perseverance. • Not at all • To a small extent • To some extent • To a moderate extent • To a great extent	2020, 2021	Developed for current survey
Sense of stability. • Not at all • To a small extent • To some extent • To a moderate extent • To a great extent	2020, 2021	Developed for current survey
Please indicate the extent to which you agree with each of the following statements.		
I have people in my life whom I can turn to for emotional support. • Strongly agree • Agree • Neither agree nor disagree • Disagree • Strongly disagree	2020, 2021	Angel, 2020
I have lasting, positive relationships. • Strongly agree • Agree • Neither agree nor disagree • Disagree • Strongly disagree	2020, 2021	Angel, 2020
I have people in my life whom I trust. • Strongly agree • Agree • Neither agree nor disagree • Disagree • Strongly disagree	2020, 2021	Angel, 2020
I have people in my life who are not my relatives but feel like family. • Strongly agree • Agree • Neither agree nor disagree • Disagree • Strongly disagree	2020, 2021	Angel, 2020
I have close, best-friend types of relationships. • Strongly agree • Agree • Neither agree nor disagree • Disagree • Strongly disagree	2020, 2021	Angel, 2020
I have people in my life whom I can turn to for information. • Strongly agree • Agree • Neither agree nor disagree • Disagree • Strongly disagree	2020, 2021	Angel, 2020

Table A.1—continued

Survey Item	Years Fielded	Sources
I feel loved. • Strongly agree • Agree • Neither agree nor disagree • Disagree • Strongly disagree	2020, 2021	Angel, 2020
I have people in my life whom I can turn to for resources (such as financial resources, help with childcare, transportation, employment). • Strongly agree • Agree • Neither agree nor disagree • Disagree • Strongly disagree	2020, 2021	Angel, 2020
I have people in my life who inspire me. • Strongly agree • Agree • Neither agree nor disagree • Disagree • Strongly disagree	2020, 2021	Angel, 2020
I feel close to another person because of a hardship we have shared together. • Strongly agree • Agree • Neither agree nor disagree • Disagree • Strongly disagree	2020, 2021	Angel, 2020
I feel a sense of accountability to others. • Strongly agree • Agree • Neither agree nor disagree • Disagree • Strongly disagree	2020, 2021	Angel, 2020
I have a sense of direction in my life. • Strongly agree • Agree • Neither agree nor disagree • Disagree • Strongly disagree	2020, 2021	Angel, 2020
I have purpose in my life. • Strongly agree • Agree • Neither agree nor disagree • Disagree • Strongly disagree	2020, 2021	Angel, 2020
I have personal goals that I am working on achieving. • Strongly agree • Agree • Neither agree nor disagree • Disagree • Strongly disagree	2020, 2021	Angel, 2020
I am optimistic and hopeful about the future. • Strongly agree • Agree • Neither agree nor disagree • Disagree • Strongly disagree	2020, 2021	Angel, 2020

Table A.1—continued

Survey Item	Years Fielded	Sources
I am proud of myself. • Strongly agree • Agree • Neither agree nor disagree • Disagree • Strongly disagree	2020, 2021	Angel, 2020
I approach life with excitement and energy. • Strongly agree • Agree • Neither agree nor disagree • Disagree • Strongly disagree	2020, 2021	Angel, 2020
I feel part of something bigger than myself. • Strongly agree • Agree • Neither agree nor disagree • Disagree • Strongly disagree	2020, 2021	Angel, 2020
I am working toward a common goal with other people. • Strongly agree • Agree • Neither agree nor disagree • Disagree • Strongly disagree	2020, 2021	Angel, 2020
My role in my family, work, or community is a positive source of self-worth and connection to others. • Strongly agree • Agree • Neither agree nor disagree • Disagree • Strongly disagree	2020, 2021	Angel, 2020
I am grateful for people or opportunities in my life. • Strongly agree • Agree • Neither agree nor disagree • Disagree • Strongly disagree	2020, 2021	Angel, 2020
I am kind and understanding toward myself when I am going through a hard time. • Strongly agree • Agree • Neither agree nor disagree • Disagree • Strongly disagree	2020, 2021	Angel, 2020
I am open-minded to trying new experiences. • Strongly agree • Agree • Neither agree nor disagree • Disagree • Strongly disagree	2020, 2021	Angel, 2020
I feel like a leader in my community. • Strongly agree • Agree • Neither agree nor disagree • Disagree • Strongly disagree	2020, 2021	Angel, 2020

Table A.1—continued

Survey Item	Years Fielded	Sources
I participate in community service activities that increase my sense of purpose. • Strongly agree • Agree • Neither agree nor disagree • Disagree • Strongly disagree	2020, 2021	Angel, 2020
I participate in leadership activities that increase my sense of purpose. • Strongly agree • Agree • Neither agree nor disagree • Disagree • Strongly disagree	2020, 2021	Angel, 2020
I feel connected to my local community. • Strongly agree • Agree • Neither agree nor disagree • Disagree • Strongly disagree	2020, 2021	Angel, 2020
I feel a sense of belonging to a larger community. • Strongly agree • Agree • Neither agree nor disagree • Disagree • Strongly disagree	2020, 2021	Angel, 2020
I put time and effort into helping others. • Strongly agree • Agree • Neither agree nor disagree • Disagree • Strongly disagree	2020, 2021	Angel, 2020
How enriched (i.e., filled with health, genuine relationships, and sense of individual and shared purpose) would you say your life is? • Very enriched • Quite enriched • Somewhat enriched • Not very enriched • Not at all enriched	2020, 2021	Angel, 2020

Please indicate how much you currently agree with each of the following statements.

Survey Item	Years Fielded	Sources
The Dog Tag Inc. Fellowship experience continues to make a positive contribution to my professional life. • Strongly agree • Agree • Neither agree nor disagree • Disagree • Strongly disagree	2020, 2021	Adapted from previous DTI alumni survey
The Dog Tag Inc. Fellowship experience continues to make a positive contribution to my personal life. • Strongly agree • Agree • Neither agree nor disagree • Disagree • Strongly disagree	2020, 2021	Adapted from previous DTI alumni survey

Table A.1—continued

Survey Item	Years Fielded	Sources
The Dog Tag Inc. Fellowship helped me to take the next steps to pursue my personal goals. • Strongly agree • Agree • Neither agree nor disagree • Disagree • Strongly disagree	2020, 2021	Developed for current survey
The Dog Tag Inc. Fellowship helped me to clarify my professional goals. • Strongly agree • Agree • Neither agree nor disagree • Disagree • Strongly disagree	2020, 2021	Developed for current survey
I feel more confident in the decisions I make about my professional life than I did prior to starting the Dog Tag Inc. Fellowship. • Strongly agree • Agree • Neither agree nor disagree • Disagree • Strongly disagree	2020, 2021	Developed for current survey
The Dog Tag Inc. Fellowship gave me the tools I needed to seek new professional opportunities. • Strongly agree • Agree • Neither agree nor disagree • Disagree • Strongly disagree	2020, 2021	Developed for current survey
As a result of the Dog Tag Inc. Fellowship, I feel excited about my professional prospects. • Strongly agree • Agree • Neither agree nor disagree • Disagree • Strongly disagree	2020, 2021	Developed for current survey
The Dog Tag Inc. Fellowship helped me chart a path that builds on my strengths. • Strongly agree • Agree • Neither agree nor disagree • Disagree • Strongly disagree	2020, 2021	Developed for current survey
The Dog Tag Inc. Fellowship helped me to approach my professional life in a more flexible way. • Strongly agree • Agree • Neither agree nor disagree • Disagree • Strongly disagree	2020, 2021	Developed for current survey
The Dog Tag Inc. Fellowship increased my access to new career paths. • Strongly agree • Agree • Neither agree nor disagree • Disagree • Strongly disagree	2020, 2021	Developed for current survey

Table A.1—continued

Survey Item	Years Fielded	Sources
As a result of the Dog Tag Inc. Fellowship, I feel comfortable working in non-military settings. • Strongly agree • Agree • Neither agree nor disagree • Disagree • Strongly disagree	2020, 2021	Developed for current survey
The Dog Tag Inc. Fellowship experience provided tools, resources, or community connections I used to get through the pandemic. • Strongly agree • Agree • Neither agree nor disagree • Disagree • Strongly disagree	2021	Developed for current survey
I feel like I have a professional mission. • Strongly agree • Agree • Neither agree nor disagree • Disagree • Strongly disagree	2020, 2021	Developed for current survey
Are you currently engaged in work, education, or volunteering that serves:		
your local community? • Yes • No	2020, 2021	Developed for current survey
the larger community of veterans, their families, and/or caregivers? • Yes • No	2020, 2021	Developed for current survey
Are you currently working on a business idea? • Yes • No	2020, 2021	Adapted from previous DTI alumni survey
(If yes) Is it the business idea you were working on as a fellow? • Yes • No	2020, 2021	Developed for current survey
What is your primary focus now? Please rank the following in order of focus, with your primary focus ranked as 1. (If you include an "Other" option, rank categories 1 through 4. If you do not include the "Other" option, rankings may include just the first three categories, ranked 1 through 3.) ___ Career/employment ___ Education ___ Personal well-being ___ Overcoming COVID-related challenges ___ Other	2020, 2021 (note: COVID-19 response option asked in 2021 only)	Adapted from previous DTI alumni survey
Which Dog Tag Inc. alumni activities have you participated in during the last 12 months? • Engagement with fellows during orientation and graduation weeks • Recruitment support • Mentorship • Professional development support from Dog Tag Inc. alumni, staff, or board • Social gatherings/networking • Personal support from DTI Staff or Board • Other (please specify): _____ • None	2020	Previous DTI alumni survey

Table A.1—continued

Survey Item	Years Fielded	Sources
Which Dog Tag Inc. alumni activities have you participated in during the last 12 months? Please check all that apply. • Engagement with fellows during orientation and graduation weeks • Alumni check-in calls and social events • Alumni interviews with candidates for Fellowship • Community connections to help address COVID-related stress or challenges • Attending events on behalf of DTI • Bakery volunteering • Voices of Dog Tag (VODT) • Mentorship program • Advisorship program • Professional development support from Dog Tag Inc. alumni, staff, or board • Personal support from DTI Staff or Board • Other (please specify): _____ • None	2021	Revised from 2020 survey
What challenges to pursuing your goals have you experienced since completing the fellowship? Please check all that apply. • Unfair treatment due to my personal characteristics, such as race, gender, or the intersection of those characteristics • My own physical or behavioral health conditions • My family's physical or behavioral health conditions • My caregiver responsibilities • Managing family needs • Lack of understanding of veteran, spouse, or caregiver needs in the workplace • Lack of understanding of veterans, spouse, or caregiver skills in the workplace • Disruptions in my work history • Relationship challenges • Current credit status or lack of savings • Challenges securing funding for my business • Concerns about maintaining my disability benefits • Challenges making connections with people • Changing geographic locations • COVID-related challenges • Other (please specify): _____ • None	2020, 2021 (note: COVID-19 response option asked in 2021 only)	Developed for current survey
How satisfied or dissatisfied are you with your experience during the Dog Tag Inc. Fellowship? • Extremely satisfied • Satisfied • Neither satisfied nor dissatisfied • Dissatisfied • Extremely dissatisfied	2020, 2021	Adapted from previous DTI alumni survey
On a scale of 0 to 10, how likely are you to recommend this fellowship to a friend or a colleague? • 0 • 1 • 2 • 3 • 4 • 5 • 6 • 7 • 8 • 9 • 10	2020, 2021	Adapted from NICE Satmetrix, 2017
Do you have any additional feedback about your experience in any aspect of the fellowship program or as an alumnus?	2020, 2021	Previous DTI alumni survey

NOTE: GED = General Educational Development.

Alumni Survey Development

Prior to the beginning of our work, Dog Tag Inc. had fielded three waves of an alumni survey, approximately six months apart (mid-2018, end of 2018, mid-2019). Although the alumni survey had provided some insights into the aspects of the program that alumni perceive to have been most influential on their personal and professional lives, DTI staff were concerned that the existing items did not capture the full impacts of the program on participants. DTI worked with RAND from 2019 to 2020 to revise the existing alumni survey to more closely align with the long-term aspirations and impacts that DTI has on the professional and personal lives of its alumni. This appendix describes the process of revising the alumni survey.

Survey Revision Methods

To revise the alumni survey, we first identified potential gaps in the current survey through multiple approaches.

Review of Dog Tag Inc. Logic Model

To begin, we conducted a crosswalk of the existing survey with the original fellowship logic model created by DTI to understand which outcomes were represented, which outcomes were not represented, and which survey items were not clearly tied to the logic model. The logic model was developed earlier in the program's operations and does not fully reflect evolutions in the program's model and goal; however, it provided an initial baseline for understanding what elements of the model were being measured and in what way. Although most logic model concepts were broadly represented on the survey, there were some limitations to the questions. For example, emotional well-being and wellness—including self-acceptance, purpose in life, and positive relationships—were identified as expected outcomes of the logic model. However, the primary well-being measures on the survey were the five-question Mental Health Inventory (MHI-5; Berwick et al., 1991), which focuses on symptoms of mental health disorders, and the Satisfaction with Life Scale (SWLS; Diener et al., 1985), which provides a fairly broad measure of satisfaction. These measures are less useful for providing insight into change in such domains as personal growth, which is not measured by these instruments but was described as a key outcome of the fellowship.

Analysis of Prior Waves of Survey Data

To revise the survey, we also drew on our analysis of the data from the original survey. This helped us to identify survey items that were difficult to interpret (e.g., because the phrasing made it challenging to pinpoint the influence of the fellowship on an outcome). For example, one question asks respondents, "Which program component had the most impact on your professional life?" If the response to this item changed from wave to wave for a given respondent, the phrasing of the item would make it unclear whether the change in response reflected a difference in the perception of the program, a change in the aspects of the program that continue to influence the individual's life (e.g., a certain program component might have more influence at different points in an alumni's post-fellowship experience), or some combination of both. In turn, this would make it difficult for DTI to know how to use the results of this item for program evaluation and improvement.

Review of Qualitative Data

The qualitative analysis also was key to informing the survey revisions. The interviews provided insight into more-specific areas of professional and personal functioning that are affected by the DTI fellowship and were not being measured directly on the survey. This included domains related to personal well-being, such as sense of purpose or self-acceptance. It also included the broader types of impact that DTI has on one's professional life, including the ability to approach one's professional life more flexibly and creatively.

Using these sources, we identified several potential revisions to the survey. As described, these included the removal of certain items or domains that no longer reflect the current DTI program model and the addition of new candidate measures that could be used to better assess the impact of the fellowship. Some new items were derived from validated measures identified through the literature, with an emphasis on measures that have been used in a variety of populations (including both veteran and nonveteran populations). Other items were developed specifically for this survey, with item prompts and response options informed by the qualitative findings.

Input from Dog Tag Inc. Staff and Cognitive Testing

As a final step, we engaged in an iterative review process with DTI to obtain feedback on potential additions and deletions. Through this process, we developed a revised survey. To test the revised survey, we conducted cognitive testing in May 2020. DTI staff facilitated outreach to a sample of five diverse fellows. Participants received a $15 Amazon gift card. Participants were asked to complete the survey draft in advance and to time themselves while completing the survey. During the cognitive interview, we asked participants to explain the meaning of each question in their own words and to elaborate on whether the available response options met their reality. In addition, we asked alumni to describe how their answers might have changed as a result of the COVID-19 pandemic.

Revised Survey

The revised version of the survey was fielded in November 2020. We conducted interim analyses and presented them to Dog Tag Inc. in spring 2021. Prior to the survey fielding period in November 2021, we reviewed the survey with the Dog Tag Inc. team to identify any additional opportunities for revision and to ensure that the survey findings would be useful for program evaluation purposes. Based on DTI's input, we made a handful of additional revisions to the survey. The complete revised survey appears in Appendix A. In this section, we detail the main changes to the survey from the version fielded in 2018 and 2019.

New Survey Items and Revisions

New additions to the survey include items in the following domains:

- **Employment status:** An item was added to assess individual income, in addition to household income, which will allow DTI to more directly assess the impact of the fellowship on the individual participating. Asking this question at baseline and completion of the fellowship would allow DTI to assess change over time. We also added two items to assess underemployment; these items address whether the individual is working in a job that does not fully use that person's education or training and whether the individual is working part-time but wants full-time work (Payscale, undated-b). For the 2020 survey, following feedback from cognitive testing, we added response options to the employment status question to assess whether a respondent is currently self-employed. These were refined in 2021 based on feedback from DTI and a desire to more explicitly identify individuals who identified as "entrepreneurs," not just "self-employed."

- **Education and/or training received:** The survey fielded in 2020 asked about the highest level of education achieved, which can be compared with baseline data to determine whether there has been a change. However, some alumni have pursued additional certifications that might not result in a subsequent degree. Therefore, we added questions to indicate whether an alumnus completed additional education—including a degree, certificate, or training program—since completing the fellowship and whether the fellowship influenced that person's decision to do so.

- **Support accessed:** The previous version of the survey included a question asking alumni about support services accessed in the past month and six months, with multiple detailed response options (e.g., VA physical health and mental health services, other veterans service organization physical and mental health services). Informed by discussions with DTI and the qualitative findings, we determined that a narrower question about sources of support *learned about through DTI* would provide a better gauge of the "ecosystem" of services that alumni use. In 2020, new response options were added to focus on fellowships or training programs offered by veteran- and non-veteran-specific organizations, with options for the respondent to specify organizations with which they interacted. In 2021, we added an additional response option to identify alumni who had used Wounded Warrior Project resources or programming.

- **Satisfaction with employment and education:** We retained six items from the original alumni survey assessing whether individuals feel satisfied with their current employment and/or postsecondary educational pursuits; feel fulfilled by their employment or educational program; and feel comfortable advocating for themselves in these roles. Drawing on the cognitive testing, we modified the question about advocating for oneself by providing examples of what that might look like in practice. We also added items to capture work-life and school-life balance. Finally, we added language to clarify that postsecondary education programs could include certificate- and non-degree-granting training programs.

- **Personal well-being:** The previous version of the survey did not specifically measure several aspects of well-being that the fellowship affects. Drawing on the qualitative data and discussions with DTI, we identified certain well-being outcomes to assess more directly, including sense of purpose, genuine relationships, personal growth, and self-acceptance. We developed a two-pronged approach to measuring these outcomes. First, we included items from the Sense of Purpose and Genuine Relationships subscales of the Enriched Life Scale (Angel et al., 2020), a measure developed by personnel from Team Red, White & Blue, a veterans service organization, and validated in a sample of veterans and civilians. A global one-item question from this scale also was included. This type of measure could be administered by DTI at baseline and completion of the fellowship to examine changes over time. Scores could also be compared with the validation sample.[1] Second, we developed a small number of items to assess perceptions of the fellowship's effect on six constructs, including personal growth and self-acceptance.

- **Engaged citizenship:** DTI aims for alumni to contribute to their communities. To better assess engaged citizenship, we included items from the Engaged Citizenship subscale of the Enriched Life Scale (Angel

---

[1]   We reviewed multiple existing, validated scales for the measurement of these well-being constructs. Our selection was guided by the fit between the way each scale operationalized the construct of interest (e.g., personal growth) and the DTI fellowship, as well as the validation samples for each scale.

et al., 2020). As with the other subscales of this measure, these items could be administered by DTI at baseline and completion of the fellowship to examine change over time.

- **Impact on professional life:** The previous version of the survey asked alumni to indicate the specific skills that they felt had improved as a result of the fellowship, including professional, communications, and development and marketing skills. Discussions with DTI staff indicated that they believe they have received useful information from these items but are interested in expanding to understand the types of effects that alumni described in the qualitative interviews (e.g., approaching professional life more flexibly, more confidence in decisionmaking). We added six items to assess the effect of the fellowship on one's professional life and goals more broadly.

- **Challenges since completing fellowship:** During the qualitative interviews, alumni discussed certain ongoing challenges affecting their professional lives, personal lives, or both. These include physical and behavioral health conditions (both one's own conditions and those of family members), difficulties encountered in the workplace, and relationship challenges. DTI expressed interest in better assessing these challenges to understand how to support fellows and alumni. An item was added to assess post-fellowship challenges. Response options were shaped by qualitative findings and cognitive testing.

- **Alumni activities:** The original DTI alumni survey had a question assessing the types of alumni activities that respondents had participated in during the past 12 months. The original options were retained for the 2020 survey, but were revised for the 2021 survey based on input from Dog Tag Inc. staff and updates to the offerings for alumni.

- **Impact of COVID-19:** During our cognitive testing process, fellows raised the point that their responses at the time of the testing were potentially quite different from what they would have been just ten weeks earlier because of the impact of the COVID-19 pandemic. Given the long-term effects that the COVID-19 pandemic likely will have on the lives of participants, we added questions to the 2020 survey to assess the extent to which fellows' personal and professional lives have been affected. These questions include two questions adapted from the Pew Research Center (Pew Research Center, 2020). For the 2021 survey, we decided to eliminate these broad COVID-19-related items, but we did add COVID-19-related response options to certain items:

  - On the underemployment question, we included the option, "I am underemployed due to the effect of the COVID-19 pandemic."
  - An item was added to determine how much alumni agreed with the following statement: "The Dog Tag Inc. Fellowship experience provided tools, resources, or community connections I used to get through the pandemic."
  - For the question asking alumni to rank their primary focus, we added "Overcoming COVID-related challenges" as an option.
  - For the question regarding alumni activities, we added "Community connections to help address COVID-related stress or challenges" as a response option.
  - For the question related to challenges to pursuing goals, we added "COVID-related challenges" as a response option.

Survey Administration

Based on input from RAND, DTI moved from administering the alumni survey every six months to every year. This decision was based on the length of the survey and the fact that, of the 34 individuals who completed the first survey, only 22 completed the second survey (a loss of 35 percent of respondents), and 15 of those completed the third survey (a loss of an additional 32 percent of respondents, compared with the second survey). Of the 18 new respondents at Wave 2, only 12 completed the third survey (a 33-percent loss).

Administering the survey less frequently has the potential to improve response rates (National Research Council, 2013).

The alumni survey is administered online, with participants invited via email. DTI provided the contact information and basic demographic information about respondents, and the survey was fielded by the RAND Survey Research Group. The survey was open for approximately one month, with weekly reminder emails. Participants received a $15 gift card for completing the survey. Some of these procedures reflected a change from the original alumni survey. For example, for that survey, participants received an initial email invitation and a reminder email sent ten days later. Email invitations were personalized to each recipient, using information collected by DTI. Certain background information (e.g., contact information, military history) was preloaded from recipients' existing data, with questions asked only if certain pieces of information were missing. However, during cognitive testing, interviewees noted that some alumni might not feel comfortable being completely truthful in their responses because of the close relationship between program staff and alumni and because responses were linked to individual participants. This informed our decision to have RAND administer the survey. In addition, participants were assured that their responses would be held confidential, with a unique study ID being assigned by RAND rather than having their contact information associated with their responses.

We hypothesized that these steps might increase the response rate for the alumni survey, which ranged from 51 percent to 55 percent for the original survey administered in 2018 and 2019. However, we found that the response rate did not change substantially, with 67 individuals completing the survey in 2020 (55-percent response rate) and 87 completing the survey in 2021 (57-percent response rate).

Data Corresponding to Chapter 5 Figures

In Table C.1, we present the complete, mutually exclusive employment status categories.

TABLE C.1

Employment Status, Combined Categories

Employment Status Category	2020 Survey Respondents (*N* = 67) *n*	2021 Survey Respondents (*N* = 87) *n*
FT employed, company	19	14
FT employed, company | Any education	1	2
FT employed, company | PT employed, company | Unemployed	1	N/A
FT employed, company | PT self-employed/entrepreneur	1	3
FT employed, company | PT self-employed/entrepreneur | Any education	1	N/A
FT employed, company | PT self-employed/entrepreneur | Volunteer	1	N/A
FT employed, company | Volunteer | Any education	N/A	1
PT employed, company	4	7
PT employed, company | Any education	2	2
PT employed, company | PT self-employed/entrepreneur | Any education	N/A	1
PT employed, company | PT self-employed/entrepreneur | Volunteer | Any education	N/A	1
PT employed, company | Unemployed	N/A	1
PT employed, company | Volunteer	1	N/A
FT self-employed/self-employed/entrepreneur	7	8
FT self-employed/entrepreneur | Any education	N/A	3
FT self-employed/entrepreneur | Unemployed	N/A	1
FT self-employed/entrepreneur | Volunteer	1	N/A
PT self-employed/entrepreneur	3	5
PT self-employed/entrepreneur | Any education	1	2

Table C.1—continued

Employment Status Category	2020 Survey Respondents (*N* = 67) *n*	2021 Survey Respondents (*N* = 87) *n*
PT self-employed/entrepreneur | Unemployed	N/A	1
PT self-employed/entrepreneur | Unemployed | Volunteer | Any education	N/A	1
PT self-employed/entrepreneur | Volunteer	N/A	2
Unemployed	14	14
Unemployed | Any education	2	4
Unemployed | Volunteer	2	2
Unemployed | Volunteer | Any education	N/A	2
Volunteer	4	2
Volunteer | Any education	N/A	1
Any education	2	7

NOTES: FT = full-time; PT = part-time, N/A = not applicable. Some respondents appear to have selected both an employment-related option and "unemployed" when they responded to this item. We were unable to determine whether this was an error on the part of the respondents or an intentional selection, and therefore we report the original responses in this table without changes made by the research team.

The data for Figure 5.2 are presented in Table C.2.

TABLE C.2

Perceptions of Current Job for 2020 and 2021 Surveys

Characteristic	2020 Survey Respondents (N = 43) % (n)	2021 Survey Respondents (N = 55) % (n)
Satisfaction with current job		
Extremely satisfied	30.2% (13)	27.3% (15)
Satisfied	41.9% (18)	41.8% (23)
Neither satisfied nor dissatisfied	14.0% (6)	23.6% (13)
Dissatisfied	7.0% (3)	7.3% (4)
Extremely dissatisfied	7.0% (3)	0.0% (0)
Fulfillment from work		
Extremely fulfilling	30.2% (13)	27.3% (15)
Fulfilling	41.9% (18)	38.2% (21)
Neither fulfilling nor unfulfilling	18.6% (8)	30.9% (17)
Unfulfilling	7.0% (3)	3.6% (2)
Extremely unfulfilling	2.3% (1)	0.0% (0)
Comfort advocating for self		
Extremely comfortable	32.6% (14)	18.2% (10)
Comfortable	46.5% (20)	50.9% (28)
Neither comfortable nor uncomfortable	20.9% (9)	23.6% (13)
Uncomfortable	0.0% (0)	7.3% (4)
Extremely uncomfortable	0.0% (0)	0.0% (0)
Satisfaction with work/life balance		
Extremely satisfied	18.6% (8)	9.1% (5)
Satisfied	44.2% (19)	56.4% (31)
Neither satisfied nor dissatisfied	16.3% (7)	14.5% (8)
Dissatisfied	18.6% (8)	16.4% (9)
Extremely dissatisfied	2.3% (1)	3.6% (2)

The data for Figure 5.3 are presented in Table C.3.

TABLE C.3

Perceptions of Postsecondary Education Experiences for 2020 and 2021 Surveys

Characteristic	2020 Survey Respondents ($N = 9$) % (n)	2021 Survey Respondents ($N = 27$) % (n)
Satisfaction with current educational experience		
Extremely satisfied	22.2% (2)	22.2% (2)
Satisfied	44.4% (4)	51.9% (14)
Neither satisfied nor dissatisfied	22.2% (2)	18.5% (5)
Dissatisfied	11.1% (1)	3.7% (1)
Extremely dissatisfied	0.0% (0)	3.7% (1)
Fulfillment from educational experience		
Extremely fulfilling	22.2% (2)	14.8% (4)
Fulfilling	55.6% (5)	66.7% (18)
Neither fulfilling nor unfulfilling	11.1% (1)	11.1% (3)
Unfulfilling	0.0% (0)	0.0% (0)
Extremely unfulfilling	11.1% (1)	0.0% (0)
Comfort advocating for self		
Extremely comfortable	33.3% (3)	18.5% (5)
Comfortable	33.3% (3)	66.7% (18)
Neither comfortable nor uncomfortable	0.0% (0)	14.8% (4)
Uncomfortable	33.3% (3)	0.0% (0)
Extremely uncomfortable	0.0% (0)	0.0% (0)
Satisfaction with school/life balance		
Extremely satisfied	0.0% (0)	14.8% (4)
Satisfied	55.6% (5)	51.9% (14)
Neither satisfied nor dissatisfied	22.2% (2)	14.8% (4)
Dissatisfied	22.2% (2)	14.8% (4)
Extremely dissatisfied	0.0% (0)	3.7% (1)

The data for Figure 5.4 are presented in Tables C.4 and C.5.

TABLE C.4
Ongoing Impact of Dog Tag Inc. Fellowship for 2020 Survey Respondents

Characteristic	Not at All	To a Small Extent	To Some Extent	To a Moderate Extent	To a Great Extent
Personal growth	13.4% (9)	11.9% (8)	26.9% (18)	19.4% (13)	28.4% (19)
Self-acceptance	17.9% (12)	7.5% (5)	23.9% (16)	19.4% (13)	31.3% (21)
Finding a sense of identity	16.4% (11)	14.9% (10)	23.9% (16)	17.9% (12)	26.9% (18)
Ability to self-reflect	7.5% (5)	10.4% (7)	28.4% (19)	26.9% (18)	26.9% (18)
Perseverance ($N = 66$)	12.1% (8)	12.1% (8)	25.8% (17)	15.2% (10)	34.8% (23)
Sense of stability	16.4% (11)	14.9% (10)	34.3% (23)	16.4% (11)	17.9% (12)

NOTE $N = 67$.

TABLE C.5
Ongoing Impact of Dog Tag Inc. Fellowship for 2021 Survey Respondents

Characteristic	Not at all	To a Small Extent	To Some Extent	To a Moderate Extent	To a Great Extent
Personal growth	6.9% (6)	13.8% (12)	28.7% (25)	25.3% (22)	25.3% (22)
Self-acceptance	8.0% (7)	13.8% (12)	32.2% (28)	21.8% (19)	24.1% (21)
Finding a sense of identity	5.7% (5)	18.4% (16)	28.7% (25)	25.3% (22)	21.8% (19)
Ability to self-reflect	9.2% (8)	18.4% (16)	26.4% (23)	19.5% (17)	26.4% (23)
Perseverance	5.7% (5)	18.4% (16)	31.0% (27)	16.1% (14)	28.7% (25)
Sense of stability ($N = 86$)	12.8% (11)	16.3% (14)	29.1% (25)	26.7% (23)	15.1% (13)

NOTE: $N = 87$.

The data for Figures 5.5, 5.6, and 5.7 are presented in Tables C.6 and C.7.

TABLE C.6

Perceived Effect of Dog Tag Inc. Fellowship on Personal and Professional Life for 2020 Survey

Characteristic	Strongly Agree	Agree	Neither Agree nor Disagree	Disagree	Strongly Disagree
The Dog Tag Inc. Fellowship experience continues to make a positive contribution to my professional life.	39.1% (25)	31.3% (20)	20.3% (13)	9.4% (6)	0.0% (0)
The Dog Tag Inc. Fellowship experience continues to make a positive contribution to my personal life.	31.3% (20)	43.8% (28)	17.2% (11)	7.8% (5)	0.0% (0)
The Dog Tag Inc. Fellowship helped me to take the next steps to pursue my personal goals.	45.3% (29)	29.7% (19)	20.3% (13)	1.6% (1)	3.1% (2)
The Dog Tag Inc. Fellowship helped me to clarify my professional goals.	43.8% (28)	35.9% (23)	17.2% (11)	3.1% (2)	0.0% (0)
I feel more confident in the decisions I make about my professional life than I did prior to starting the Dog Tag Inc. Fellowship.	50.0% (32)	31.3% (20)	15.6% (10)	1.6% (1)	1.6% (1)
The Dog Tag Inc. Fellowship gave me the tools I needed to seek new professional opportunities.	43.8% (28)	43.8% (28)	10.9% (7)	1.6% (1)	0.0% (0)
As a result of the Dog Tag Inc. Fellowship, I feel more excited about my professional prospects.	37.5% (24)	32.8% (21)	20.3% (13)	9.4% (6)	0.0% (0)
The Dog Tag Inc. Fellowship helped me chart a path that builds on my strengths.	34.4% (22)	42.2% (27)	17.2% (11)	4.7% (3)	1.6% (1)
The Dog Tag Inc. Fellowship helped me to approach my professional life in a more flexible way.	37.5% (24)	39.1% (25)	12.5% (8)	10.9% (7)	0.0% (0)
The Dog Tag Inc. Fellowship increased my access to new career paths.	35.9% (23)	37.5% (24)	20.3% (13)	6.3% (4)	0.0% (0)
As a result of the Dog Tag Inc. Fellowship, I feel comfortable working in nonmilitary settings.	32.8% (21)	29.7% (19)	31.3% (20)	6.3% (4)	0.0% (0)
I feel like I have a professional mission.	34.4% (22)	32.8% (21)	21.9% (14)	9.4% (6)	1.6% (1)

NOTE: $N = 64$.

TABLE C.7

Perceived Effect of Dog Tag Inc. Fellowship on Personal and Professional Life for 2021 Survey

Characteristic	Strongly Agree	Agree	Neither Agree nor Disagree	Disagree	Strongly Disagree
The Dog Tag Inc. Fellowship experience continues to make a positive contribution to my professional life. (N = 85)	37.6% (32)	41.2% (35)	20.0% (17)	1.2% (1)	0.0% (0)
The Dog Tag Inc. Fellowship experience continues to make a positive contribution to my personal life.	28.2% (24)	51.7% (44)	17.6% (15)	2.4% (2)	0.0% (0)
The Dog Tag Inc. Fellowship helped me to take the next steps to pursue my personal goals.	41.9% (36)	45.3% (39)	12.8% (11)	0.0% (0)	0.0% (0)
The Dog Tag Inc. Fellowship helped me to clarify my professional goals.	40.7% (35)	45.3% (39)	12.8% (11)	1.2% (1)	0.0% (0)
I feel more confident in the decisions I make about my professional life than I did prior to starting the Dog Tag Inc. Fellowship.	44.2% (38)	38.4% (33)	15.1% (13)	2.3% (2)	0.0% (0)
The Dog Tag Inc. Fellowship gave me the tools I needed to seek new professional opportunities.	41.9% (36)	45.3% (39)	12.8% (11)	0.0% (0)	0.0% (0)
As a result of the Dog Tag Inc. Fellowship, I feel more excited about my professional prospects.	41.9% (36)	36.0% (31)	18.6% (16)	3.5% (3)	0.0% (0)
The Dog Tag Inc. Fellowship helped me chart a path that builds on my strengths.	34.9% (30)	46.5% (40)	16.3% (14)	2.3% (2)	0.0% (0)
The Dog Tag Inc. Fellowship helped me to approach my professional life in a more flexible way.	41.9% (36)	40.7% (35)	17.4% (15)	0% (0)	0.0% (0)
The Dog Tag Inc. Fellowship increased my access to new career paths. (N = 85)	41.2% (35)	40.0% (34)	15.3% (13)	3.5% (3)	0.0% (0)
As a result of the Dog Tag Inc. Fellowship, I feel comfortable working in nonmilitary settings. (N = 85)	31.8% (27)	41.2% (35)	24.7% (21)	2.4% (2)	0.0% (0)
I feel like I have a professional mission.	31.4% (27)	39.5% (34)	20.9% (18)	7.0% (6)	1.2% (1)

NOTE: N = 86.

The data for Figure 5.8 are presented in Table C.8.

TABLE C.8

Perceived Effect of Dog Tag Inc. Fellowship on Personal and Professional Life for 2021 Survey—Additional COVID-19 Question

Characteristic	Strongly Agree	Agree	Neither Agree nor Disagree	Disagree	Strongly Disagree
The Dog Tag Inc. Fellowship provided resources to navigate COVID-19.	29.1% (25)	38.4% (33)	20.9% (18)	10.5% (9)	1.2% (1)

NOTE: N = 86.

The data for Figure 5.9 are presented in Table C.9.

TABLE C.9

Enriched Life Scale Scores for 2020 and 2021 Survey Waves

Subscore	2020 Survey Wave (N = 67)			2021 Survey Wave (N = 87)		
	Mean (*SD*)	Range	Cronbach's Alpha	Mean (*SD*)	Range	Cronbach's Alpha
Genuine Relationships	82.97 (15.14)	45.45, 100.00	0.91	79.05 (15.5)	38.64, 100.00	0.96
Sense of Purpose	75.75 (17.97)	29.17, 100.00	0.94	71.95 (17.63)	29.17, 100.00	0.94
Engaged Citizenship	63.28 (21.66)	16.67, 100.00	0.89	61.92 (21.18)	8.33, 100.00	0.90
Enrichment Score	66.04 (25.26)	0.00, 100.00	-	64.71 (22.92)	0.00, 100.00	-

NOTE: The three subscales had good internal consistency (Cronbach's alpha for Genuine Relationships was 0.91 in 2020 and 0.96 in 2021; for Sense of Purpose was 0.94 in 2020 and 2021; and for Engaged Citizenship was 0.89 in 2020 and 0.90 in 2021).

The data for Figures 5.10, 5.11, and 5.12 are presented in Table C.10.

TABLE C.10

Post-Fellowship Experiences for 2020 and 2021 Surveys

Characteristic	2020 Survey Responses N = 65-67 % (*n*)	2021 Survey Responses N = 85–87 % (*n*)
Pursued additional education since fellowship (*N* = 67; *N* = 87)	56.7% (38)	69.0% (60)
Decision influenced by fellowship	63.2% (24)	68.3% (41)
Engaged in work, education, or volunteering that serves local community (*N* = 67; *N* = 85)	53.8% (36)	55.3% (47)
Engaged in work, education, or volunteering that serves community of veterans, families, and/or caregivers (*N* = 34; *N* = 85)	40.0% (34)	44.7% (38)
Working on a business idea (*N* = 65; *N* = 86)	52.3% (34)	58.1% (50)
Business idea working on as fellow	52.9% (18)	58.0% (29)

The data for Figures 5.13 and 5.14 are presented in Table C.11.

TABLE C.11
Alumni Engagement for 2020 and 2021 Surveys

Alumni Activity	2020 Survey Responses (N = 65) % (n)	2021 Survey Responses (N = 86) % (n)
One or more alumni activity[a]	68.8% (44)	72.1% (62)
Social gatherings/ networking	44.6% (29)	–
Alumni check-in calls and social events	–	57.0% (49)
Personal support from DTI Staff or Board	30.8% (20)	16.3% (14)
Engagement with fellows during orientation/graduation weeks	26.2% (17)	30.2% (26)
Professional development events with guest speakers outside DTI	21.5% (14)	–
Professional development support from DTI alumni, staff, or board	21.5% (14)	14.0% (12)
Recruitment support	20.0% (13)	–
Alumni interviews with candidates for Fellowship	–	19.8% (17)
Attending events on behalf of DTI	–	16.3% (14)
Voices of Dog Tag (VODT)	–	10.5% (9)
Mentorship to recent graduates	18.5% (12)	–
Mentorship program	–	29.1% (25)
Other[b]	6.2% (4)	9.3% (8)
Advisorship program	3.1% (2)	9.3% (8)
Community connections to help address COVID-19 related stress or challenges	–	7.0% (6)
Bakery volunteering	–	2.3% (2)
None	–	24.4% (21)

NOTE: Item was "check all that apply," so categories do not necessarily add up to 100%.

[a] Respondents reporting participating in one or more of the alumni activities (excluding the responses to the "other" category).

[b] Other responses for 2020 included informal connections, alumni calls and interviews, election day. Other responses for 2021 included sharing the work about DTI to the military community (spouses, warriors, etc.); personal growth and friendship with alumni; partnerships with other nonprofits; volunteering for other alumni projects; "love by the DTI familia"; project advising.

The data for Figure 5.15 are presented in Table C.12.

TABLE C.12

Respondents Current Focus from 2020 Survey

	Number Who Ranked This Item	Ranked 1st	Ranked 2nd	Ranked 3rd	Ranked 4th
Career	$N = 65$	29.2% (19)	30.8% (20)	28.1% (18)	29.6% (8)
Education	$N = 61$	16.9% (11)	18.5% (12)	45.3% (29)	33.3% (9)
Personal well-being	$N = 64$	40.0% (26)	41.5% (27)	15.6% (10)	3.7% (1)
Other[a]	$N = 31$	13.8% (9)	9.2% (6)	10.9% (7)	33.3% (9)

NOTE: $N = 66$.

[a] Other included family, financial well-being, health, service, and other personal and professional goals.

The data for Figure 5.16 are presented in Table C.13.

TABLE C.13

Respondents Current Focus from 2021 Survey

	Number Who Ranked This Item	Ranked 1st	Ranked 2nd	Ranked 3rd	Ranked 4th	Ranked 5th
Career	$N = 85$	31.4% (27)	23.3% (20)	33.7% (29)	8.1% (7)	2.3% (2)
Education	$N = 85$	14.0% (12)	32.6% (28)	23.3% (20)	25.6% (22)	3.5% (3)
Personal well-being	$N = 86$	44.2% (38)	24.4% (21)	23.3% (20)	7.0% (6)	1.2% (1)
COVID-19 related challenges	$N = 79$	1.2% (1)	14.0% (5)	12.8% (5)	46.5% (40)	17.4% (15)
Other[a]	$N = 31$	9.3% (8)	5.8% (5)	5.8% (5)	10.5% (9)	4.7% (4)

NOTE: $N = 86$.

[a] Other responses included family, VA claims, health, personal life changes (wedding, moving, etc.), travel, and spirituality.

The data for Figure 5.17 are presented in Table C.14.

TABLE C.14

Challenges to Pursuing Goals from 2020 and 2021 Surveys

Challenge	2020 Survey Respondents (N = 64) % (n)	2021 Survey Respondents (N = 86) % (n)
Own physical or behavioral health conditions	51.6% (33)	50.0% (43)
Managing family needs	43.8% (28)	45.4% (39)
Relationship challenges	35.9% (23)	34.9% (30)
Changing geographic locations	31.3% (20)	20.9% (18)
Disruptions in work history	29.7% (19)	20.9% (18)
Family's physical or behavioral health conditions	28.1% (18)	34.9% (30)
Challenges maintaining connections with people	25.0% (16)	36.1% (31)
Other[a]	23.4% (15)	14.0% (12)
Caregiver responsibilities	23.4% (15)	18.6% (16)
Challenges securing funding for my business	17.2% (11)	19.8% (17)
Current credit status or lack of savings	17.2% (11)	14.0% (12)
Concerns about maintaining my disability benefits	15.6% (10)	14.0% (12)
Lack of understanding of needs in the workplace	14.1% (9)	10.5% (9)
Unfair treatment due to personal characteristics	10.9% (7)	14.0% (12)
Lack of understanding of skills in the workplace	9.4% (6)	10.5% (9)
COVID-19 related challenges[b]	–	33.7% (29)
None	4.7% (3)	2.3% (2)

NOTE: Item was "check all that apply," so categories do not necessarily add up to 100%.

[a] Other responses included need more financial resources; toxic work environment; need additional education; divorcing service member and now disconnected from the supportive military community; gaining access to DoD and VA benefits; lost medical insurance coverage; transitioning out of military (spouse, self); transportation; opportunities in the geographic location are limited.

[b] Question new to the 2021 survey.

The data for Figure 5.18 are presented in Table C.15.

TABLE C.15

Respondents Overall Satisfaction with Dog Tag Inc. Fellowship by Survey Wave

	2018 Wave 1 (*N* = 34) % (*n*)	2018 Wave 2 (*N* = 41) % (*n*)	2019 Survey Responses (*N* = 51) % (*n*)	2020 Survey Responses (*N* = 64) % (*n*)	2021 Survey Responses (*N* = 86) % (*n*)
Extremely satisfied	70.6% (24)	82.5% (33)	78.4% (40)	71.9% (46)	70.9% (61)
Satisfied	23.5% (8)	15.0% (6)	15.7% (8)	23.4% (15)	24.4% (21)
Neither satisfied nor dissatisfied	0.0% (0)	2.5% (1)	5.9% (3)	3.1% (2)	3.5% (3)
Dissatisfied	5.9% (2)	0.0% (1)	0.0% (0)	1.6% (1)	1.2% (1)
Extremely dissatisfied	0.0% (0)	0.0% (0)	0.0% (0)	0.0% (0)	0% (0)

Analyses from the Original Dog Tag Inc. Alumni Survey (2018 and 2019)

Under a previous contract, RAND conducted a secondary analysis of the data from the first three waves of the alumni survey, which were fielded in 2018 and 2019. In this appendix, we present findings from that survey.

Participants

Wave 1 of the survey included participants from Cohorts 1 through 7 ($n = 34$ respondents; 51-percent response rate); Wave 2 of the survey included participants from Cohorts 1 through 8 ($n = 40$; 51-percent response rate); and Wave 3 of the survey included participants from Cohorts 1 through 9 ($n = 51$; 55-percent response rate). A total of 38 individuals participated in all three waves of the survey; 21 participated in two waves; and 15 participated in a single wave. There were very few missing responses on variables of interest. Table D.1 summarizes the demographic characteristics of respondents in each wave.

TABLE D.1

Sociodemographic Characteristics of Respondents by Survey Wave

Characteristic	Wave 1 Respondents (N = 34) % (n)	Wave 2 Respondents (N = 40) % (n)	Wave 3 Respondents (N = 51) % (n)
Military status			
Military only	79.4% (27)	70.0% (28)	62.7% (32)
Spouse only	8.8% (3)	10.0% (4)	15.7% (8)
Caregiver only	2.9% (1)	2.5% (1)	2.0% (1)
Linguist only	0.0% (0)	2.5% (1)	2.0% (1)
Veteran and spouse	5.9% (2)	7.5% (3)	9.8% (5)
Spouse and caregiver	2.9% (1)	7.5% (3)	5.9% (3)
Veteran, spouse, and caregiver	0.0% (0)	0.0% (0)	2.0% (1)
Employment status[a]			
Full-time employed (32+ hours per week)	35.3% (12)	40.0% (16)	29.4% (15)
Part-time employed (<32 hours per week)	17.6% (6)	17.5% (7)	33.3% (17)
Unemployed	23.5% (8)	32.5% (13)	31.4% (16)

Table D.1—continued

Characteristic	Wave 1 Respondents (N = 34) % (n)	Wave 2 Respondents (N = 40) % (n)	Wave 3 Respondents (N = 51) % (n)
Volunteer	26.5% (9)	10.0% (4)	17.6% (9)
Full-time postsecondary education	14.7% (5)	7.5% (3)	7.8% (4)
Part-time postsecondary education	8.8% (3)	12.5% (5)	9.8% (5)
In military transition (still active duty)	5.9% (2)	0.0% (0)	2.0% (1)
Highest level of education			
High school	0.0% (0)	2.5% (1)	3.9% (2)
Some college	11.8% (4)	10.0% (4)	7.8% (4)
Associate's degree	14.7% (5)	10.0% (4)	9.8% (5)
Bachelor's degree	38.2% (13)	37.5% (15)	43.1% (22)
Master's degree or higher	32.4% (11)	40.0% (16)	33.3% (17)
Other	0.0% (0)	0.0% (0)	2.0% (1)
Income			
$35,000 or less	2.9% (1)	7.5% (3)	9.8% (5)
$35,001–$50,000	8.8% (3)	12.5% (5)	5.9% (3)
$50,001–$75,000	17.6% (6)	37.5% (15)	21.6% (11)
$75,001–$100,000	20.6% (7)	17.5% (7)	19.6% (10)
$100,001–$150,000	11.8% (4)	5.0% (2)	25.5% (13)
$150,001–$250,000	11.8% (4)	12.5% (5)	7.8% (4)
More than $250,001	0.0% (0)	2.5% (1)	2.0% (1)
Prefer not to answer	0.0% (0)	5.0% (2)	7.8% (4)
Marital status			
Single	29.4% (10)	30.0% (12)	23.5% (12)
Married	52.9% (18)	52.5% (21)	64.7% (33)
Living with partner	11.8% (4)	10.0% (4)	5.9% (3)
Other	5.9% (2)	7.5% (3)	5.9% (3)
Location			
DMV	67.6% (23)	70.0% (28)	72.5% (37)
Other than DMV	32.4% (11)	30.0% (12)	27.5% (14)
Cohort			
Cohort 1	—	—	—
Cohort 2	8.8% (3)	7.5% (3)	7.8% (4)
Cohort 3	11.8% (4)	12.5% (5)	5.9% (3)

Table D.1—continued

Characteristic	Wave 1 Respondents (*N* = 34) % (*n*)	Wave 2 Respondents (*N* = 40) % (*n*)	Wave 3 Respondents (*N* = 51) % (*n*)
Cohort 4	14.7% (5)	10.0% (4)	13.7% (7)
Cohort 5	11.8% (4)	10.0% (4)	11.8% (6)
Cohort 6	20.6% (7)	15.0% (6)	13.7% (7)
Cohort 7	32.4% (11)	17.5% (7)	7.8% (4)
Cohort 8	N/A	27.5% (11)	11.8% (6)
Cohort 9	N/A	N/A	27.5% (14)

SOURCE: RAND analysis of DTI alumni surveys.

NOTES: N/A = not applicable; indicates that a cohort was not in existence at the time of a particular survey wave. A dash (—) indicates that there were no responses. There are small numbers of individuals in certain categories, which increases the likelihood that their identities could be inferred. Because DTI has access to these survey data in identifiable form, and this report is for internal purposes only, we have opted to report the small numbers of respondents in certain categories. For a public report, we would combine certain categories and/or avoid presenting variables or categories that could lead to an individual being identified by inference.

[a] Categories are not mutually exclusive.

Satisfaction with Current Job or Postsecondary Education Experience

Participants responded to a series of questions related to their current job (or most recent job, if currently unemployed), as well as their current postsecondary education experience. Although there were slight variations in responses at each wave, the majority of respondents at each wave reported that they are moderately or extremely satisfied with their current job and find their job to be fulfilling (Table D.2). Most respondents indicated that they feel extremely comfortable advocating for their needs at work.

TABLE D.2

Perceptions of Current Job by Survey Wave

Characteristic	Wave 1 Respondents (*N* = 30) % (*n*)	Wave 2 Respondents (*N* = 37) % (*n*)	Wave 3 Respondents (*N* = 50) % (*n*)
Satisfaction with current job			
Extremely satisfied	26.7% (8)	32.4% (12)	28.0% (14)
Moderately satisfied	30.0% (9)	24.3% (9)	40.0% (20)
Slightly satisfied	3.3% (1)	18.9% (7)	10.0% (5)
Neither satisfied nor dissatisfied	20.0% (6)	16.2% (6)	12.0% (6)
Slightly dissatisfied	10.0% (3)	2.7% (1)	0.0% (0)
Moderately dissatisfied	10.0% (3)	0.0% (0)	8.0% (4)
Extremely dissatisfied	0.0% (0)	5.4% (2)	2.0% (1)
Current job is fulfilling			
Extremely fulfilling	30.0% (9)	35.1% (13)	34.0% (17)
Moderately fulfilling	40.0% (12)	32.4% (12)	38.0% (19)
Slightly fulfilling	0.0% (0)	10.8% (4)	8.0% (4)
Neither fulfilling nor unfulfilling	10.0% (3)	16.2% (6)	12.0% (6)

Table D.2—continued

Characteristic	Wave 1 Respondents (N = 30) % (n)	Wave 2 Respondents (N = 37) % (n)	Wave 3 Respondents (N = 50) % (n)
Slightly unfulfilling	6.7% (2)	0.0% (0)	2.0% (1)
Moderately unfulfilling	6.7% (2)	0.0% (0)	6.0% (3)
Extremely unfulfilling	6.7% (2)	5.4% (2)	0.0% (0)
Comfort advocating for needs at work			
Extremely comfortable	46.7% (14)	35.1% (13)	44.0% (22)
Moderately comfortable	20.0% (6)	27.0% (10)	34.0% (17)
Slightly comfortable	13.3% (4)	13.5% (5)	8.0% (4)
Neither comfortable nor uncomfortable	10.0% (3)	13.5% (5)	10.0% (5)
Slightly uncomfortable	3.3% (1)	2.7% (1)	2.0% (1)
Moderately uncomfortable	6.7% (2)	2.7% (1)	2.0% (1)
Extremely uncomfortable	0.0% (0)	5.4% (2)	0.0% (0)

SOURCE: RAND analysis of DTI alumni surveys.

NOTE: The proportion responding to these questions is somewhat lower than the overall sample because only those individuals who were employed answered questions about their current job, and only those enrolled in postsecondary education answered questions about their educational experience.

Given that few alumni were pursuing postsecondary education, a smaller subset of participants responded to education-focused questions (Table D.3). However, the majority responded to the employment-focused questions. The majority reported feeling satisfied with their current educational experience, finding their experience fulfilling, and feeling comfortable advocating for their needs in their educational setting. We did not conduct subgroup analyses for this set of questions because of the small number of respondents who answered the questions at each wave.

TABLE D.3

Perceptions of Current Postsecondary Educational Experience by Survey Wave

Characteristic	Wave 1 Respondents (N = 8) % (n)	Wave 2 Respondents (N = 8) % (n)	Wave 3 Respondents (N = 9) % (n)
Satisfaction with current educational experience			
Extremely satisfied	25.0% (2)	37.5% (3)	33.3% (3)
Moderately satisfied	62.5% (5)	50.0% (4)	33.3% (3)
Slightly satisfied	12.5% (1)	0.0% (0)	11.1% (1)
Neither satisfied nor dissatisfied	0.0% (0)	0.0% (0)	22.2% (2)
Slightly dissatisfied	0.0% (0)	2.5% (1)	0.0% (0)
Moderately dissatisfied	0.0% (0)	0.0% (0)	0.0% (0)
Extremely dissatisfied	0.0% (0)	0.0% (0)	0.0% (0)
Current educational experience is fulfilling			
Extremely fulfilling	37.5% (3)	37.5% (3)	33.3% (3)
Moderately fulfilling	50.0% (4)	50.0% (4)	44.4% (4)
Slightly fulfilling	12.5% (1)	0.0% (0)	0.0% (0)
Neither fulfilling nor unfulfilling	0.0% (0)	2.5% (1)	22.2% (2)
Slightly unfulfilling	0.0% (0)	0.0% (0)	0.0% (0)
Moderately unfulfilling	0.0% (0)	0.0% (0)	0.0% (0)
Extremely unfulfilling	0.0% (0)	0.0% (0)	0.0% (0)
Comfort advocating for needs in educational setting			
Extremely comfortable	62.5% (5)	62.5% (5)	44.4% (4)
Moderately comfortable	25.0% (2)	25.0% (2)	22.2% (2)
Slightly comfortable	0.0% (0)	0.0% (0)	11.1% (1)
Neither comfortable nor uncomfortable	12.5% (1)	12.5% (1)	11.1% (1)
Slightly uncomfortable	0.0% (0)	0.0% (0)	11.1% (1)
Moderately uncomfortable	0.0% (0)	0.0% (0)	0.0% (0)
Extremely uncomfortable	0.0% (0)	0.0% (0)	0.0% (0)

SOURCE: RAND analysis of DTI alumni surveys.

NOTE: The proportion responding to these questions is somewhat lower than the overall sample because only those individuals who were employed answered questions about their current job, and only those enrolled in postsecondary education answered questions about their educational experience.

Contributions of Fellowship to Professional Life, Personal Life, and Community Engagement

Across waves, most participants agreed or strongly agreed that the fellowship positively contributed to their professional lives (Table D.4). At Waves 1 and 2, participants endorsed the business administration courses as having the most impact on their professional lives, whereas they identified the Learning Lab sessions as most impactful at Wave 3.

TABLE D.4

Contributions of Fellowship to Alumni Professional Life by Survey Wave

Characteristic	Wave 1 Respondents % (n)	Wave 2 Respondents % (n)	Wave 3 Respondents % (n)
Fellowship positively contributed to professional life			
Strongly agree	58.8% (20)	57.5% (23)	60.8% (31)
Agree	32.4% (11)	32.5% (13)	29.4% (15)
Slightly agree	5.9% (2)	5.0% (2)	5.9% (3)
Neither agree nor disagree	2.9% (1)	5.0% (2)	3.9% (2)
Slightly disagree	0.0% (0)	0.0% (0)	0.0% (0)
Disagree	0.0% (0)	0.0% (0)	0.0% (0)
Strongly disagree	0.0% (0)	0.0% (0)	0.0% (0)
Program component with most impact on professional life			
Business administration courses	**47.1% (16)**	**35.0% (14)**	37.3% (19)
Experiential learning rotations	14.7% (5)	25.0% (10)	7.8% (4)
Learning Lab sessions	20.6% (7)	15.0% (6)	**39.2% (20)**
Capstone project	14.7% (5)	10.0% (4)	9.8% (5)
Wellness activities	2.9% (1)	5.0% (2)	3.9% (2)
Finding Your Voice	0.0% (0)	10.0% (4)	2.0% (1)

SOURCE: RAND analysis of DTI alumni surveys.

NOTE: Top endorsed domains for each wave are in bold type.

Most participants across waves indicated that the fellowship positively contributed to their personal life (Table D.5). Across waves, respondents indicated that Finding Your Voice was the program component with the most impact on their personal life. There was some slight variation in responses by cohort; for example, respondents from Cohorts 3 and 6 indicated that wellness activities had the most impact on their personal life.

TABLE D.5

Contributions of Fellowship to Alumni Personal Life by Survey Wave

Characteristic	Wave 1 Respondents % (n)	Wave 2 Respondents % (n)	Wave 3 Respondents % (n)
Fellowship positively contributed to personal life			
Strongly agree	58.8% (20)	57.5% (23)	56.9% (29)
Agree	26.5% (9)	35.0% (14)	33.3% (17)
Slightly agree	8.8% (3)	2.5% (1)	5.9% (3)
Neither agree nor disagree	5.9% (2)	5.0% (2)	3.9% (2)
Slightly disagree	0.0% (0)	0.0% (0)	0.0% (0)
Disagree	0.0% (0)	0.0% (0)	0.0% (0)
Strongly disagree	0.0% (0)	0.0% (0)	0.0% (0)
Program component with most impact on personal life			
Business administration courses	0.0% (0)	2.5% (1)	0.0% (0)
Experiential learning rotations	11.8% (4)	7.5% (3)	5.9% (3)
Learning Lab sessions	17.6% (6)	30.0% (12)	11.8% (6)
Capstone project	2.9% (1)	5.0% (2)	0.0% (0)
Wellness activities	26.5% (9)	17.5% (7)	39.2% (20)
Finding Your Voice	**41.2% (14)**	**37.5% (15)**	**43.1% (22)**

SOURCE: RAND analysis of DTI alumni surveys.

NOTE: Top endorsed domains for each wave are in bold type.

Respondents were asked to indicate which skills have improved through their fellowship (Table D.6). In Wave 1, 77 percent of respondents indicated that their personal skills had improved and 74 percent indicated that their communication skills had improved. In Wave 2, the largest proportion of respondents indicated that professional and communication skills had improved (83 percent for each). In Wave 3, the largest proportion of respondents indicated that their professional skills had improved (71 percent), followed by communication skills (69 percent).

Regarding subgroup analyses, there was some variation observed across cohorts. Respondents from Cohorts 2 and 6 consistently endorsed an effect on professional skills; those from Cohort 4 consistently endorsed an effect on communication skills; those from Cohort 6 consistently endorsed an effect on operations skills; and those from Cohorts 5 and 6 consistently endorsed an effect on personal skills. Analyses by location found that, consistent with the overall findings, professional, communication, and personal skills were endorsed most often.

TABLE D.6
Skills That Have Improved Through the Fellowship by Survey Wave

Characteristic	Wave 1 Respondents % (n)	Wave 2 Respondents % (n)	Wave 3 Respondents % (n)
Professional skills	61.8% (21)	**82.5% (33)**	**70.6% (36)**
Communication skills	73.5% (25)	**82.5% (33)**	68.6% (35)
Operations	52.9% (18)	52.5% (21)	45.1% (23)
Development and marketing	55.9% (19)	47.5% (19)	47.1% (24)
Finance and strategy	50.0% (17)	55.0% (22)	39.2% (20)
Personal skills	**76.5% (26)**	**82.5% (33)**	64.7% (33)

SOURCE: RAND analysis of DTI alumni surveys.

NOTE: Top endorsed domains for each wave are in bold type.

The DTI fellowship aims to promote participant engagement in their communities. The majority of respondents across waves indicated that they participate in their communities and give back (Table D.7). There was little variation by cohort or location.

TABLE D.7
Community Engagement by Survey Wave

Characteristic	Wave 1 Respondents % (n)	Wave 2 Respondents % (n)	Wave 3 Respondents % (n)
Strongly agree	32.4% (11)	22.5% (9)	21.6% (11)
Agree	32.4% (11)	27.5% (11)	35.3% (18)
Slightly agree	17.6% (6)	22.5% (9)	21.6% (11)
Neither agree nor disagree	8.8% (3)	12.5% (5)	13.7% (7)
Slightly disagree	5.9% (2)	2.5% (1)	5.9% (3)
Disagree	0.0% (0)	10.0% (4)	2.0% (1)
Strongly disagree	2.9% (1)	2.5% (1)	0.0% (0)

SOURCE: RAND analysis of DTI alumni surveys.

Satisfaction with the Fellowship

Nearly all alumni reported being moderately to extremely satisfied with the fellowship (Table D.8). There did not appear to be substantial differences by cohort or location.

TABLE D.8

Overall Satisfaction with the Fellowship by Survey Wave

Characteristics	Wave 1 Respondents % (n)	Wave 2 Respondents % (n)	Wave 3 Respondents % (n)
Extremely satisfied	70.6% (24)	82.5% (33)	78.4% (40)
Moderately satisfied	23.5% (8)	12.5% (5)	15.7% (8)
Slightly satisfied	0.0% (0)	2.5% (1)	0.0% (0)
Neither satisfied nor dissatisfied	5.9% (2)	2.5% (1)	5.9% (3)
Slightly dissatisfied	0.0% (0)	0.0% (0)	0.0% (0)
Moderately dissatisfied	0.0% (0)	0.0% (0)	0.0% (0)
Extremely dissatisfied	0.0% (0)	0.0% (0)	0.0% (0)

SOURCE: RAND analysis of DTI alumni surveys.

Mental Health and Well-Being

The survey included the MHI-5 (Berwick et al., 1991). On this scale, higher scores indicate better mental health, and scores can range from 0 to 100. Some research has found that scores above 76 are generally associated with better mental health in community populations (Kelly et al., 2008). This scale had good internal consistency across waves (Cronbach's alpha = 0.84 to 0.88).

Scores across the three waves ranged from approximately 62 to 64, suggesting that DTI alumni might continue to experience higher rates of mental health concerns than are experienced in the general population (Table D.9). Other studies have used a somewhat more liberal cutoff of 60 (Kelly et al., 2008), but even when this cutoff is used, alumni scores are near the threshold.

Well-being was measured with the SWLS (Diener et al., 1985). Scores correspond to the following categories: extremely satisfied (31–35); satisfied (26–30); slightly satisfied (21–25); neutral (20); slightly dissatisfied (15–19); dissatisfied (10–14); and extremely dissatisfied (5–9). This scale also had good internal consistency

TABLE D.9

Mental Health and Well-Being Scores by Survey Wave

Measure	Wave 1 Respondents M (SD)	Wave 2 Respondents M (SD)	Wave 3 Respondents M (SD)
Mental health (MHI-5 score)	62.35 (20.35)	61.60 (21.58)	63.69 (19.10)
	Range = 16–92	Range = 12–96	Range = 20–92
Well-being (SWLS score)	24.21 (7.78)	23.00 (7.64)	24.33 (6.69)
	Range = 5–35	Range = 5–35	Range = 5–35

SOURCE: RAND analysis of DTI alumni surveys.

NOTE: SD = standard deviation.

across waves (Cronbach's alpha = 0.90 to 0.93). Across waves, the average scores on this scale fell into the *slightly satisfied* range (Table D.9).

There were slight variations by cohort across waves on these measures, but small sample sizes within cohorts make it difficult to interpret these differences. Scores were generally consistent by location across waves.

Summary

These analyses provide some insight into the experiences of DTI alumni, including the aspects of the program that had the most impact on their personal and professional lives, satisfaction with current jobs and postsecondary educational experiences, and mental health and well-being. However, there are certain limitations to these survey data that should be kept in mind. First, a relatively small number of individuals participated in each survey, and an even smaller subset of those respondents participated across multiple survey waves, making it difficult to more formally explore changes over time. Second, there are limitations in our ability to understand the factors that might have driven differences in responses across each survey wave. For example, the proportion of respondents reporting satisfaction with the fellowship increased from approximately 71 percent at Wave 1 to 83 percent at Wave 2, but it is difficult to determine what might account for this increase. (For example, was it a change in the perceived relevance of the fellowship to respondents at that point in time? Was it a difference based on the specific individuals who responded at Wave 1 but not at Wave 2?). In addition, certain questions were worded in a way that makes it difficult to understand the ongoing impact of the fellowship. For example, the survey includes the question about which skills improved through the fellowship. However, some respondents might have answered this while thinking back to their fellowship experience, whereas others might have responded about the skills they continue to use that were developed during the fellowship. Finally, there are certain domains that the fellowship aims to address that were not reflected by the survey, such as sense of purpose and positive relationships, which provided an opportunity to revise the survey to more directly assess these outcomes.

Abbreviations

9/11	September 11, 2001
COVID-19	coronavirus disease 2019
DMV	Washington, D.C., Maryland, and Virginia
DTI	Dog Tag Inc.
MHI-5	Mental Health Inventory–5
PTSD	posttraumatic stress disorder
SD	standard deviation
SWLS	Satisfaction with Life Scale
TBI	traumatic brain injury
VA	U.S. Department of Veterans Affairs
VSO	veteran service organization
WWP	Wounded Warrior Project

References

Ainspan, Nathan D., Walter Penk, and Lisa K. Kearney, "Psychosocial Approaches to Improving the Military-to-Civilian Transition Process," *Psychological Services*, Vol. 15, No. 2, May 2018, pp. 129–134.

American Psychological Association and Harris Interactive, *Workplace Survey: American Psychological Association*, Washington, DC, 2012. Accessed April 25, 2022: https://cdn2.hubspot.net/hub/54367/file-1347675125-pdf/docs/apaworkplacesurvey.pdf?t=1434041041881

Angel, Caroline M., Blayne P. Smith, John M. Pinter, Brandon B. Young, Nicholas J. Armstrong, Joseph P. Quinn, Daniel F. Brostek, David E. Goodrich, Katherine D. Hoerster, and Michael S. Erwin, "Team Red, White & Blue: A Community-Based Model for Harnessing Positive Social Networks to Enhance Enrichment Outcomes in Military Veterans Reintegrating to Civilian Life," *Translational Behavioral Medicine*, Vol. 8, No. 4, July 17, 2018, pp. 554–564.

Angel, Caroline M., Mahlet A. Woldetsadik, Nicholas J. Armstrong, Brandon B. Young, Rachel K. Linsner, Roslainda V. Maury, and John M. Pinter, "The Enriched Life Scale (ELS): Development, Exploratory Factor Analysis, and Preliminary Construct Validity for U.S. Military Veteran and Civilian Samples," *Translational Behavioral Medicine*, Vol. 10, No. 1, February 3, 2020, pp. 278–291.

Avila, Daniela Dean, and Kurt G. Lunsford, *Underemployment Following the Great Recession and the COVID-19 Recession*, Cleveland, Ohio: Federal Reserve Bank of Cleveland, No. 2022-01, February 3, 2022.

Becker, Karen, Adelle Bish, Matthew McCormack, and Dan Abell, "Reconceptualizing Identities: Veterans' Perspectives on Career Transition Challenges," *Human Resource Development Quarterly*, January 31, 2022.

Berwick, Donald M., Jane M. Murphy, Paula A. Goldman, John E. Ware, Jr., Arthur J. Barsky, and Milton C. Weinstein, "Performance of a Five-Item Mental Health Screening Test," *Medical Care*, Vol. 29, No. 2, 1991, pp. 169–176.

Biniecki, Susan M. Yelich, and Paul Berg, "The Senior Military Officer as a Veteran in Transition: Opportunities for Adult Learning and Bridging the Military–Civilian Divide," *New Directions for Adult & Continuing Education*, Vol. 2020, No. 166, June 2020, pp. 25–36.

Bommarito, Rachael K., Michelle D. Sherman, Jessie H. Rudi, Jude P. Mikal, and Lynne M. Borden, "Challenges Facing Military Spouses During Postdeployment Reintegration: A Review of the Literature and Current Supports," *Military Behavioral Health*, Vol. 5, No. 1, 2017, pp. 51–63.

Bonawitz, Kirsten, Marisa Wetmore, Michele Heisler, Vanessa K. Dalton, Laura J. Damschroder, Jane Forman, Katie R. Allan, and Michelle H. Moniz, "Champions in Context: Which Attributes Matter for Change Efforts in Healthcare?" *Implementation Science*, Vol. 15, No. 1, 2020, p. 62.

Bond, Gary R., Monirah Al-Abdulmunem, Daniel R. Ressler, Robert E. Drake, Lori L. Davis, Thomas Meyer, Daniel M. Gade, B. Christopher Frueh, and Ross B. Dickman, "Evaluation of an Employment Intervention for Veterans Transitioning From the Military: A Randomized Controlled Trial," *Journal of Nervous and Mental Disease*, Vol. 210, No. 5, May 2022, pp. 321–329.

Boros, Paula, and Kara S. Erolin, "Women Veterans after Transition to Civilian Life: An Interpretative Phenomenological Analysis," *Journal of Feminist Family Therapy*, Vol. 33, No. 4, 2021, pp. 330–353.

Borsari, Brian, Ali Yurasek, Mary Beth Miller, James G. Murphy, Meghan E. McDevitt-Murphy, Matthew P. Martens, Monica G. Darcy, and Kate B. Carey, "Student Service Members/Veterans on Campus: Challenges for Reintegration," *American Journal of Orthopsychiatry*, Vol. 87, No. 2, 2017, pp. 166–175.

Botero, Gabriel, Jr., Nilsa I. Rivera, Shakeya C. Calloway, Pedro L. Ortiz, Emily Edwards, John Chae, and Joseph C. Geraci, "A Lifeline in the dark: Breaking Through the Stigma of Veteran Mental Health and Treating America's Combat Veterans," *Journal of Clinical Psychology*, Vol. 76, No. 5, 2020, pp. 831–840.

Butler-Kisber, Lynn, *Qualitative Inquiry: Thematic, Narrative and Arts-Informed Perspectives*: Sage Publications, 2010.

Center on Budget and Policy Priorities, *The COVID-19 Economy's Effects on Food, Housing, and Employment Hardships*, Washington, D.C.: Center on Budget and Policy Priorities, 2021.

Chazdon, Scott, Mary Emery, Debra Hansen, Lorie Higgins, and Rebecca Sero, *A Field Guide to Ripple Effects Mapping*, Minneapolis, Minn.: University of Minnesota Libraries Publishing, 2017.

Copeland, Laurel A., Erin P. Finley, Dwayne Vogt, Daniel F. Perkins, and Yael I. Nillni, "Gender Differences in Newly Separated Veterans' Use of Healthcare," *American Journal of Managed Care*, Vol. 26, No. 3, March 2020, pp. 97–104.

Coursera, *2021 Impact Report: Serving the World Through Learning*, Mountain View, Calif., 2021.

Davis, Lori L., Catherine M. Blansett, Mercy N. Mumba, David MacVicar, Richard Toscano, Patricia Pilkinton, Whitney Gay, and Aal Bartolucci, "The Methods and Baseline Characteristics of a VA Randomized Controlled Study Evaluating Supported Employment Provided in Primary Care Patient Aligned Care Teams," *BMC Medical Research Methodology*, Vol. 20, Article 33, February 17, 2020.

Demers, Anne, "When Veterans Return: The Role of Community in Reintegration," *Journal of Loss & Trauma*, Vol. 16, No. 2, 2011, pp. 160–179.

Derefinko, Karen J., Troy A. Hallsell, Matthew B. Isaacs, Lauren W. Colvin, Francisco I. Salgado Garcia, and Zoran Bursac, "Perceived Needs of Veterans Transitioning from the Military to Civilian Life," *Journal of Behavioral Health Services Research,* Vol. 46, No. 3, July 2019, pp. 384–398.

Dexter, John C., "Human Resources Challenges of Military to Civilian Employment Transitions," *Career Development International*, Vol. 25, No. 5, 2020, pp. 481–500.

Diener, Ed, Robert A. Emmons, Randy J. Larsen, and Sharon Griffin, "The Satisfaction with Life Scale," *Journal of Personality Assessment*, Vol. 49, 1985, pp. 71–75.

Dog Tag Inc., "Apply to the Dog Tag Fellowship Program," webpage, undated-a. Accessed April 25, 2022: https://www.dogtaginc.org/pages/application

Dog Tag Inc., "The Dog Tag Fellowship Program," webpage, undated-b. Accessed May 25, 2022: https://www.dogtaginc.org/pages/our-program

Dyar, Kelly, "Veterans as Students in Higher Education: A Scoping Review," *Nursing Education Perspectives*, Vol. 40, No. 6, November/December 2019, pp. 333–337.

Erwin, Stephanie K., "Haze Gray but Never Again Underway: The Veteran Borderlands," *New Horizons in Adult Education and Human Resource Development*, Vol. 32, No. 3, June 2020, pp. 20–34.

Flack, Mal, and Leah Kite, "Transition from Military to Civilian: Identity, Social Connectedness, and Veteran Wellbeing," *PLoS One*, Vol. 16, No. 12, 2021, p. e0261634.

Freedy, John R., Kathryn M. Magruder, Arch G. Mainous, B. Chris Frueh, Mark E. Geesey, and Mark Carnemolla, "Gender Differences in Traumatic Event Exposure and Mental Health Among Veteran Primary Care Patients," *Military Medicine*, Vol. 175, No. 10, 2010, pp. 750–758.

Gallup, "Work and Workplace," webpage, undated. Accessed April 25, 2022: https://news.gallup.com/poll/1720/work-work-place.aspx

Geraci, Joseph C., Meaghan Mobbs, Emily R. Edwards, Bryan Doerries, Nicholas Armstrong, Robert Porcarelli, Elana Duffy, Colonel Michael Loos, Daniel Kilby, Josephine Juanamarga, Gilly Cantor, Loree Sutton, Yosef Sokol, and Marianne Goodman, "Expanded Roles and Recommendations for Stakeholders to Successfully Reintegrate Modern Warriors and Mitigate Suicide Risk," *Frontiers in Psychology*, Vol. 11, Article 1907, 2020.

Gettings, Patricia E., Elizabeth Dorrance Hall, Steven R. Wilson, Daniel M. Kamal, Jill Inderstrodt-Stephens, and Linda Hughes-Kirchubel, "Effects of Reintegration Difficulties, Perceived Message Acceptance and Perceived Autonomy Support on U.S. military Veterans' Evaluations of Messages Encouraging Them to Seek Behavioral Health Care," *Communication Monographs*, Vol. 86, No. 2, 2019, pp. 205–228.

Gil-Rivas, Virginia, Ryan P. Kilmer, Jacqueline C. Larson, and Laura Marie Armstrong, "Facilitating Successful Reintegration: Attending to the Needs of Military Families," *American Journal of Orthopsychiatry*, Vol. 87, No. 2, 2017, pp. 176–184.

Goetter, Elizabeth M., Susanne S. Hoeppner, Amanda J. Khan, Meredith E. Charney, Sarah Wieman, Margaret R. Venners, Kimberly M. Avallone, Sheila A. M. Rauch, and Naomi M. Simon, "Combat-Related Posttraumatic Stress Disorder and Comorbid Major Depression in U.S. Veterans: The Role of Deployment Cycle Adversity and Social Support," *Journal of Traumatic Stress*, Vol. 33, No. 3, 2020, pp. 276–284.

Gorman, Jay A., Arielle A. J. Scoglio, John Smolinsky, Anthony Russo, and Charles E. Drebing, "Veteran Coffee Socials: A Community-Building Strategy for Enhancing Community Reintegration of Veterans," *Community Mental Health Journal*, Vol. 54, No. 8, 2018, pp. 1189–1197.

Greer, Tomika W., "Adult Learning and Development Goals for Female Veterans' Career Transitions Amid Cultural Adaptation and Identity Formation," *New Directions for Adult and Continuing Education,* Vol. 2020, No. 166, 2020, pp. 151–162.

Gregg, Brian T., Dana M. Howell, and Anne Shordike, "Experiences of Veterans Transitioning to Postsecondary Education," *American Journal of Occupational Therapy*, Vol. 70, No. 6, November/December 2016, pp. 7006250010p1–7006250010p8.

Grimell, Jan, "Making Dialogue with an Existential Voice in Transition from Military to Civilian Life," *Theory & Psychology*, Vol. 27, No. 6, December 2017, pp. 832–850.

Gumber, Clayton, and Jonathan Vespa, *The Employment, Earnings, and Occupations of Post-9/11 Veterans*, American Community Survey Reports, ACS-46, November 2020.

Harrod, Molly, Erin M. Miller, Jennifer Henry, and Kara Zivin, "'I've Never Been Able to Stay in a Job': A Qualitative Study of Veterans' Experiences of Maintaining Employment," *Work*, Vol. 57, No. 2, 2017, pp. 259–268.

Haynie, J. Michael, and Dean Shepherd, "Toward a Theory of Discontinuous Career Transition: Investigating Career Transitions Necessitated by Traumatic Life Events," *Journal of Applied Psychology*, Vol. 96, No. 3, 2011, pp. 501–524.

Heinz, Adrienne J., Michael A. Freeman, Ilan Harpaz-Rotem, and Robert H. Pietrzak, "American Military Veteran Entrepreneurs: A Comprehensive Profile of Demographic, Service History, and Psychosocial Characteristics," *Military Psychology*, Vol. 29, No. 6, 2017, pp. 513–523.

Horigian, Viviana E., Renae D. Schmidt, and Daniel J. Feaster, "Loneliness, Mental Health, and Substance Use Among US Young Adults During COVID-19," *Journal of Psychoactive Drugs,* Vol. 53, No. 1, 2021, pp. 1–9.

Hunter-Johnson, Yvonne, Yuanlu Niu, Sharlene Smith, Brandi Whitaker, Rehshetta Wells, and Aynur Charkasova, "The Veteran Employees: Recruitment, Career Development, Engagement, and Job Satisfaction of Veterans Transitioning to the Civilian Workforce," *New Directions for Adult & Continuing Education*, Vol. 2020, No. 166, Summer 2020, pp. 139–150.

Keeling, Mary, Elisa V. Borah, Sara Kintzle, Meredith Kleykamp, and Heather C. Robertson, "Military Spouses Transition Too! A Call to Action to Address Spouses' Military to Civilian Transition," *Journal of Family Social Work*, Vol. 23, No. 1, 2020, pp. 3–19.

Kelly, Mark J., Frank D. Dunstan, Keith Lloyd, and David L. Fone, "Evaluating Cutpoints for the MHI-5 and MCS Using the GHQ-12: A Comparison of Five Different Methods," *BMC Psychiatry*, Vol. 8, No. 1, February 2008, Article 10.

Kelty, Ryan, Todd Woodruff, and David R. Segal, "Relative Salience of Family Versus Soldier Role-Identity Among Combat Soldiers," in Neobi M. Karakatsanis and Jonathan Swarts, eds., *Political and Military Sociology* New York: Routledge, 2017, pp. 35–60.

Kerrick, Sharon A., Denise M. Cumberland, and Namok Choi, "Comparing Military Veterans and Civilians Responses to an Entrepreneurship Education Program," *Journal of Entrepreneurship Education*, Vol. 19, No. 1, 2016, p. 9.

Kleykamp, Meredith, Sidra Montgomery, Alexis Pang, and Kristin Schrader, "Military Identity and Planning for the Transition out of the Military," *Military Psychology*, Vol. 33, No. 6, 2021, pp. 372–391.

Knobloch, Leanne K., Erin D. Basinger, and Jennifer A. Theiss, "Relational Turbulence and Perceptions of Partner Support During Reintegration After Military Deployment," *Journal of Applied Communication Research*, Vol. 46, No. 1, 2018, pp. 52–73.

Kocchar, Rakesh, and Jesse Bennett, "U.S. Labor Market Inches Back from the COVID-19 Shock, but Recovery Is Far from Complete," Pew Research Center, April 14, 2021.

Krigbaum, Genomary, Christine C. Good, Ann K. Ogle, Michael Walsh, Robert Hess, and Jeff Krigbaum, "Factors in the Transition of Career Military Personnel to the Civilian Workforce," *TIP: The Industrial-Organizational Psychologist*, Vol. 57, No. 4, Spring 2020, pp. 51–65.

Lim, Nelson, and David Schulker, *Measuring Underemployment Among Military Spouses*, Santa Monica, Calif.: RAND Corporation, MG-918-OSD, 2010. As of May 18, 2022: https://www.rand.org/pubs/monographs/MG918.html

Link, Patrick E., and Lawrence A. Palinkas, "Long-Term Trajectories and Service Needs for military Families," *Clinical Child and Family Psychology Review*, Vol. 16, No. 4, 2013, pp. 376–393.

Linstad, Casey, and David J. Schafer, "A Marine's Journey from Battle Injury to Employment in Home Community," *Journal of Clinical Psychology*, Vol. 50, No. 1, January 18, 2020, pp. 97–102.

Mamon, Daria, Arielle A. J. Scoglio, Rachelle M. Calixte, Rivka Tuval-Mashiach, Benjamin Patton, and Charles E. Drebing, "Connecting Veterans and Their Community Through Narrative: Pilot Data on a Community Strengthening Intervention," *Community Mental Health Journal*, Vol. 56, No. 5, July 2020, pp. 804–813.

McGarity Suzanne, Scott D. Barnett, Greg Lamberty, Tracy Kretzmer, Gail Powell-Cope, Nitin Patel, and Risa Nakase-Richardson, "Community Reintegration Problems Among Veterans and Active Duty Service Members with Traumatic Brain Injury," *Journal of Head Trauma Rehabilitation*," Vol. 32, No. 1, January/February 2017, pp. 34–45.

Meadows, Sarah O., Beth Ann Griffin, Benjamin R. Karney, and Julia Pollak, "Employment Gaps Between Military Spouses and Matched Civilians," *Armed Forces & Society*, Vol. 42, No. 3, 2015, pp. 542–561.

Meca, Alan, Kelsie K. Allison, Kenneth L. Ayers, Kyla Carr, Sean Cox, Adrian J. Bravo, Rachel Davies, and Michelle L. Kelley, "Understanding the Unique Effects of Identity in Adjustment Among Veterans," *Military Behavioral Health*, Vol. 9, No. 4, 2021, pp. 1–424.

Minnis, Sarah E., "Fostering Infantry Veterans' Civilian Cultural Adaptation for Employment," *New Directions for Adult & Continuing Education*, Vol. 2020, No. 166, Summer 2020, pp. 11–24.

Morin, Rich, *The Difficult Transition from Military to Civilian Life*, Washington, D.C.: Pew Research Center, December 8, 2011.

National Research Council, "The Growing Problem of Nonresponse," in *Nonresponse in Social Science Surveys: A Research Agenda*, Washington, D.C.: National Academies Press, 2013, pp. 7–39.

NICE Satmetrix, "What Is Net Promoter? A Trusted Anchor for Your Customer Experience Management Program," webpage, 2017. As of June 10, 2020: https://www.netpromoter.com/know/

Orazem, Robert J., Patricia A. Frazier, Paula P. Schnurr, Heather E. Oleson, Kathleen F. Carlson, Brett T. Litz, and Nina A. Sayer, "Identity Adjustment Among Afghanistan and Iraq War Veterans with Reintegration Difficulty," *Psychological Trauma*, Vol. 9, No. Suppl. 1, August 2017, pp. 4–11.

Parker, Kim, and Juliana Menasche Horowitz, " Majority of Workers Who Quit a Job in 2021 Cite Low Pay, No Opportunities for Advancement, Feeling Disrespected," Pew Research Center, March 9, 2022.

Payscale, "The Underemployment Big Picture," webpage, undated-a. As of May 18, 2022: https://www.payscale.com/data-packages/underemployment

Payscale, "Underemployment Methodology," webpage, undated-b. As of April 15, 2020: https://www.payscale.com/data-packages/underemployment/methodology

Perkins, Daniel F., Katie E. Davenport, Nicole R. Morgan, Keith R. Aronson, Julia A. Bleser, Kimberly J. McCarthy, Dawne Vogt, Erin P. Finley, Laurel A. Copeland, and Cynthia L. Gilman, "The Influence of Employment Program Components upon Job Attainment During a Time of Identity and Career Transition," *International Journal for Educational and Vocational Guidance*, February 2022.

Perkins, Daniel F., Keith R. Aronson, Nicole R. Morgan, Julia A. Bleser, Dawne Vogt, Laurel A. Copeland, Erin P. Finley, and Cynthia Gilman, "Veterans' Use of Programs and Services as They Transition to Civilian Life: Baseline Assessment for the Veteran Metrics Initiative," *Journal of Social Service Research*, Vol. 46, No. 2, 2020, pp. 241–255.

Pew Research Center, *The State of American Jobs*, Washington, D.C., October 6, 2016.

Pew Research Center, *Most Americans Say Coronavirus Outbreak Has Impacted Their Lives*, Washington, D.C., March 2020.

Phelan, Sean M., Lauren R. Bangerter, Greta Friedemann-Sanchez, Kandace A. Lackore, Megan A. Morris, Courtney H. Van Houtven, Kathleen F. Carlson, Michelle van Ryn, Kristin J. Harden, and Joan M. Griffin, "The Impact of Stigma on Community Reintegration of Veterans with Traumatic Brain Injury and the Well-Being of Their Caregivers," *Archives of Physical Medicine and Rehabilitation*, Vol. 99, No. 11, November 2018, pp. 2222–2229.

Powell, Byron J., Thomas J. Waltz, Matthew J. Chinman, Laura J. Damschroder, Jeffrey L. Smith, Monica M. Matthieu, Enola K. Proctor, and JoAnn E. Kirchner, "A Refined Compilation of Implementation Strategies: Results from the Expert Recommendations for Implementing Change (ERIC) Project," *Implementation Science*, Vol. 10, Article 21, 2015.

Ramchand, Rajeev, Terri Tanielian, Michael P. Fisher, Christine Anne Vaughan, Thomas E. Trail, Caroline Epley, Phoenix Voorhies, Michael William Robbins, Eric Robinson, and Bonnie Ghosh-Dastidar, *Hidden Heroes: America's Military Caregivers*, Santa Monica, Calif.: RAND Corporation, RR-499-TEDF, 2014. As of May 18, 2022:
https://www.rand.org/pubs/research_reports/RR499.html

Ravindran, Chandru, Sybil W. Morley, Brady M. Stephens, Ian H. Stanley, and Mark A. Reger, "Association of Suicide Risk with Transition to Civilian Life Among US Military Service Members," *JAMA Network Open*, Vol. 3, No. 9, 2020.

Ringel, Rae, "When Do We Actually Need to Meet in Person?" *Harvard Business Review*, July 6, 2021.

Ryan, Gery W., and H. Russell Bernard, "Techniques to Identify Themes," *Field Methods*, Vol. 15, No. 1, 2003, pp. 85–109.

Sayer, Nina A., Robert J. Orazem, Lauren L. Mitchell, Kathleen F. Carlson, Paula P. Schnurr, and Brett T. Litz, "What the Public Should Know About Veterans Returning from Combat Deployment to Support Reintegration: A Qualitative Analysis," *American Journal of Orthopsychiatry*, Vol. 91, No. 3, 2021, pp. 398–406.

Sayer, Nina A., Siamak Noorbaloochi, Patricia A. Frazier, James W. Pennebaker, Robert J. Orazem, Paula P. Schnurr, Maureen Murdoch, Kathleen F. Carlson, Amy Gravely, and Brett T. Litz, "Randomized Controlled Trial of Online Expressive Writing to Address Readjustment Difficulties Among U.S. Afghanistan and Iraq War Veterans," *Journal of Traumatic Stress*, Vol. 28, No. 5, 2015, pp. 381–390.

Sayers, Steven L., "Family Reintegration Difficulties and Couples Therapy for Military Veterans and Their Spouses," *Cognitive and Behavioral Practice*, Vol. 18, No. 1, 2011, pp. 108–119.

Schreger, Cade, and Matthew Kimble, "Assessing Civilian Perceptions of Combat Veterans: An IAT Study," *Psychological Trauma*, Vol. 9, No. Suppl. 1, August 2017, pp. 12–18.

Schulker, David, "The Recent Occupation and Industry Employment Patterns of American Veterans," *Armed Forces and Society*, Vol. 43, No. 4, October 2017, pp. 695–710.

Senecal, Gary, "The Social Vacuum & the Loss of Solidarity for Veterans Experienced in Civilian Reintegration," *New Male Studies*, Vol. 7, No. 1, 2018, pp. 54–75.

Senecal, Gary, MaryCatherine McDonald, Richard LaFleur, and Charles Coey, "Examining the Effect of Combat Excitement & Diminished Civilian Solidarity on Life Satisfaction for American Veterans," *New Ideas in Psychology*, Vol. 52, January 2019, pp. 12–17.

Shepherd, Steven, Aaron C. Kay, and Kurt Gray, "Military Veterans Are Morally Typecast as Agentic but Unfeeling: Implications for Veteran Employment," *Organizational Behavior and Human Decision Processes*, Vol. 153, 2019, pp. 75–88.

Shepherd-Banigan, Megan, Terri K. Pogoda, Kevin McKenna, Nina Sperber, and Courtney H. Van Houtven, "Experiences of VA Vocational and Education Training and Assistance Services: Facilitators and Barriers Reported by Veterans with Disabilities," *Psychiatric Rehabilitation Journal*, Vol. 44, No. 2, 2021, pp. 148–156.

Shue, Sarah, Marianne S. Matthias, Dennis P. Watson, Kristione K. Miller, and Niki Munk, "The Career Transition Experiences of Military Veterans: A Qualitative Study," *Military Psychology*, Vol. 33, No. 6, 2021, pp. 359–371.

SocioCultural Research Consultants LLC, Dedoose, version 8.3.20, web application for managing, analyzing, and presenting qualitative and mixed method research data, Los Angeles, Calif., 2020.

Sokol, Yosef, Molly Gromatsky, Emily R. Edwards, Ashley L. Greene, Joseph C. Geraci, Rachel E. Harris, and Marianne Goodman, "The Deadly Gap: Understanding Suicide Among Veterans Transitioning out of the Military," *Psychiatry Research*, Vol. 300, 2021.

Stern, Lisa, "Post 9/11 Veterans with Service-Connected Disabilities and Their Transition to the Civilian Workforce: A Review of the Literature," *Advances in Developing Human Resources*, Vol. 19, No. 1, 2017, pp. 66–77.

Stevenson, Brian J., "Psychotherapy for Veterans Navigating the Military-to-Civilian Transition: A Case Study," *Journal of Clinical Psychology*, Vol. 76, No. 5, 2020, pp. 896–904.

Strack, Rainer, Orsolya Kovács-Ondrejkovic, Jens Baier, Pierre Antebi, Kare Kavanagh, and Ana López Gobernado, *Decoding Global Reskilling and Career Paths*, Boston, Mass.: Boston Consulting Group, 2021.

Strong, Jessica D., Brandi M. Crowe, and Sarah Lawson, "Female Veterans: Navigating Two Identities," *Clinical Social Work Journal*, Vol. 46, No. 2, 2018, pp. 92–99.

Tarbet, Zachary, Steven Moore, and Ahmed Alanazi, "Discharge, But No Exit: An Existential Qualitative Interpretive Meta-Synthesis of Veteran Reintegration," *British Journal of Social Work,* Vol. 51, No. 8, December 2021, pp. 3319–3339.

Tihic, Mirza, Muris Hadzic, and Alexander McKelvie, "Social Support and Its Effects on Self-Efficacy Among Entrepreneurs with Disabilities," *Journal of Business Venturing Insights*, Vol. 16, 2021, pp. e00279.

U.S. Bureau of Labor Statistics, "Supplemental Data Measuring the Effects of the Coronavirus (COVID-19) Pandemic on the Labor Market," webpage, 2022. Accessed April 25, 2022: https://www.bls.gov/cps/effects-of-the-coronavirus-covid-19-pandemic.htm#:~:text=Of%20the%2016.9%20 million%20people,the%20pandemic%20(78%20percent)

U.S. Department of Veterans Affairs, Veterans Health Administration, *Physical Medicine and Rehabilitation Individualized Rehabilitation and Community Reintegration Care Plan*, VHA Handbook 1172.04, Washington, D.C., 2010.

U.S. Department of Veterans Affairs, Office of Data Governance and Analytics, *Minority Veterans Report: Military Service History and VA Benefit Utilization Statistics*, Washington, D.C.: March 2017.

U.S. Department of Veterans Affairs, National Center for Veterans Analysis and Statistics, "Profile of Post-9/11 Veterans: 2016," briefing slides, March 2018.

VA—*See* U.S. Department of Veterans Affairs.

Van Bommel, T., *Remote-Work Options Can Boost Productivity and Curb Burnout*, Catalyst, 2021. As of March 22, 2022: https://www.catalyst.org/reports/remote-work-burnout-productivity/

Van Slyke, Ryan D., and Nicholas J. Armstrong, "Communities Serve: A Systematic Review of Need Assessments on U.S. Veteran and Military-Connected Populations," *Armed Forces and Society*, Vol. 46, No. 4, 2020, pp. 564–594.

Vick, Brandon, "Measuring Multi-Dimensional Deprivation Among U.S. Veterans," *Social Indicators Research*, Vol. 150, No. 1, 2020, pp. 191–218.

Vogt, Dawne, Shelby C. Borowski, Lauren R. Godier-McBard, Matt J. Fossey, Laurel A. Copeland, Daniel F. Perkins, and Erin P. Finley, "Changes in the Health and Broader Well-Being of U.S. Veterans in the First Three Years After Leaving Military Service: Overall Trends and Group Differences," *Social Science and Medicine*, Vol. 294, February 2022.

Vogt, Dawne S., Fanita A. Tyrell, Emily A. Bramande, Yael I. Nillni, Emily C. Taverna, Erin P. Finley, Danniel F. Perkins, and Laurel A. Copeland, "U.S. Military Veterans' Health and Well-Being in the First Year After Service," *American Journal of Preventive Medicine*, Vol. 58, No. 3, March 2020, pp. 352–360.

Wesselmann, Eric D., Dan Ispas, Mark D. Olson, Mark E. Swerdlik, and Natasha M. Caudle, "Does Perceived Ostracism Contribute to Mental Health Concerns Among Veterans Who Have Been Deployed?" *PLoS One*, Vol. 13, No. 12, 2018, p. e0208438.

Wewiorski, Nancy J., Jay A. Gorman, Arielle A. J. Scoglio, Seiya Fukuda, Erin Reilly, Lisa Mueller, Maureen O'Connor, Walter E. Penk, and Charles E. Drebing, "Promising Practices in Vocational Services for the Community Reintegration of Returning Veterans: The Individual Placement and Support Model and Beyond," *Psychological Services*, Vol. 15, No. 2, May 2018, pp. 191–199.

Williams, Lindsay, Carol Pavlish, Sally Maliski, and Donna Washington, "Clearing Away Past Wreckage: A Constructivist Grounded Theory of Identity and Mental Health Access by Female Veterans," *ANS: Advances in Nursing Science*, Vol. 41, No. 4, October/December 2018, pp. 327–339.